ROMAN REPUBLICAN COINS
IN THE ROYAL ONTARIO MUSEUM

To Neda Leipen, Curator Emeritus,
with deep appreciation.

ROMAN REPUBLICAN COINS
IN THE ROYAL ONTARIO MUSEUM

AND *AES RUDE,* ITALIC CAST BRONZE COINS,
AND ITALIC ISSUES FROM THE SOCIAL WAR OF 91–87 BC

ALISON HARLE EASSON

ROM
ROYAL ONTARIO MUSEUM

© 1998 Royal Ontario Museum

All rights reserved. No part of this publication may be reproduced, stored in
a retrieval system or data base, or transmitted, in any form or by any means,
without the prior written permission of the publisher or, in the case of
photocopying or other reprographic copying, a license from CANCOPY
(Canadian Reprography Collective), Toronto, Ontario.

First published in 1998 by the Royal Ontario Museum,
100 Queen's Park, Toronto, Ontario M5S 2C6

The publisher gratefully acknowledges the generosity of the J. Douglas
Ferguson Historical Research Foundation whose financial assistance made
possible the publication of this work.

Academic Editorial Board
Editor: Barbara Stephen
Associate Editor: James McDonald
Associate Editor: Janet Holmes

Manuscript Editor: Barbara Stephen
Production Editor: Lenore Gray Spence
Design: Virginia Morin
Layout: Dianna Little

Canadian Cataloguing-in-Publication Data

Royal Ontario Museum
    Roman Republican coins in the Royal Ontario Museum

Includes bibliographical references and index.
ISBN 0-88854-428-6

1. Coins, Roman - Ontario - Toronto - Catalogs. 2. Royal Ontario Museum -
Catalogs. I. Easson, Alison Harle, 1941-   . II. Title.

CJ815.C32T67 1998   737.4937'074'713541   C98-930107-9

Cover: Didrachm with janiform head of the Dioscuri.
Gift of R. E. Hindley (No. 24)

The Royal Ontario Museum is an agency of the Ontario Ministry of
Citizenship, Culture and Recreation.

Printed and bound in Canada by Transcontinental Printing Inc.

CONTENTS

ACKNOWLEDGEMENTS

The photographs were taken by Mr. William Robertson, formerly of the ROM's Photography Department, and I am grateful to him for his meticulous care in their preparation. The final prints were made by Mr. Allan McColl, of the Photography Department. The specific gravities were kindly provided by Mr. Chris Toogood of the ROM's Conservation Department. I would like to acknowledge the kindness of the two anonymous reviewers. Their corrections and amendments have been incorporated into the text. Although Reviewer B requested that the descriptions of the obverses and reverses be minimal, they have been shortened only to a certain extent. Certain necessary references are not easily obtainable in North America and it was decided that the descriptions should be more complete than Reviewer B would have wished. The legends have been given in full since they are not always very clear on the coins. I am grateful to Bruce R. Brace for reading certain sections of the catalogue and to William E. Metcalf, American Numismatic Society, for copies of pages from the catalogue for the Naville Sale IV in 1922. Michael Crawford has been very generous with his advice on certain issues. The Deutsches Archäologisches Institut, Berlin, very kindly allowed me to use the library in June 1992. The final text remains my responsibilty.

This publication was made possible through the generosity of the J. Douglas Ferguson Historical Research Foundation.

SELECT BIBLIOGRAPHY AND ABBREVIATIONS

ADOLPH HESS

(1932): Adolph Hess Nachfolger, *Römische Münzen.* Catalogue of Auction held on 9 May 1932 (Adolph Hess Nachfolger; Lucerne, 1932).

ADOLPH HESS

(1970): Adolph Hess AG and Bank Leu, *Antike Münzen.* Catalogue of Auction held on 12 and 13 May 1970 (Adolph Hess AG and Bank Leu; Lucerne, 1970).

ALFÖLDI

(1960): A. Alföldi, "Diana Nemorensis," *American Journal of Archaeology* 64 (1960) 137–44.

ALFÖLDI AND GIARD

(1984): A. Alföldi and J.-B. Giard, "Guerre civile et propagande politique: l'émission d'Octave au nom du Divos Julius (41–40 avant J.C.)," *Quaderni Ticinesi di Numismatica e Antichità Classiche* XIII (1984) 147–53.

AMANDRY

(1986): M. Amandry, "Le monnayage en bronze de Bibulus, Atratinus et Capito I," *Schweizerische Numismatische Rundschau* 65 (1986) 3–85.

AMANDRY

(1987): M. Amandry, "Le monnayage en bronze de Bibulus, Atratinus et Capito II," *Schweizerische Numismatische Rundschau* 66 (1987) 101–12.

AMANDRY

(1990): M. Amandry, "Le monnayage en bronze de Bibulus, Atratinus et Capito III," *Schweizerische Numismatische Rundschau* 69 (1990) 65–96.

ARSLAN

(1983): E. A. Arslan, *Monete Repubblicane Romana* (Musei Civici di Breschia Cataloghi 2; Brescia, 1983).

AUCTIONES

(1975): Auctiones A.G., *Auktion 5: Münzen der Antike und Neuzeit aus Privatbesitz.* Catalogue of Auction held on 2 and 3 December 1975 (Auctiones A.G.; Basel, 1975).

AUCTIONES

(1977): Auctiones A.G., *Auktion 7: Münzen der Antike und Neuzeit aus Privatbesitz.* Catalogue of Auction held on 7 and 8 June 1977 (Auctiones A.G.; Basel, 1977).

AUCTIONES

(1979): Auctiones A.G., *Auktion 10: Münzen der Antike, des Mittelalters und der Neuzeit aus Privatbesitz.* Catalogue of Auction held on 12 and 13 June 1979 (Auctiones A.G.; Basel, 1979).

AUCTIONES

(1983): Auctiones A.G., *Auktion 13: Münzen der Antike, des Mittelalters und der Neuzeit aus Privatbesitz.* Catalogue of Auction held on 23 and 24 June 1983 (Auctiones A.G.; Basel, 1983).

AUCTIONES

(1986): Auctiones A.G., *Auktion 16: Münzen der Antike, des Islams und der Neuzeit aus Privatbesitz.* Catalogue of Auction held on 1 and 2 October 1986 (Auctiones A.G.; Basel, 1986).

AUCTIONES

(1988): Auctiones A.G., *Auktion 17: Münzen der Antike und Neuzeit aus Privatbesitz.* Catalogue of Auction held on 7 and 8 June 1988 (Auctiones A.G.; Basel, 1988).

BMCRR

(1910): H. A. Grueber, *Coins of the Roman Republic in the British Museum,* 3 vols. (The Trustees; London, 1910).

BMCRR

(repr., 1970): H. A. Grueber, *Coins of the Roman Republic in the British Museum,* 3 vols. (The Trustees of the British Museum; photolithic reprint; London, 1970).

BABELON

(1885): E. Babelon, *Description historique et chronologique des monnaies de la République romaine,* 2 vols. (Paris, 1885).

BAHRFELDT

(1905): M. Bahrfeldt, "Die Münzen der Flottenpräfekten des Marcus Antonius," *Numismatische Zeitschrift* 37 (1905) 9–56.

BANK LEU

(1977): Bank Leu AG Zürich, *Auction 47: Silbermünzen der romischen Republik.* Catalogue of Auction held 3–4 May 1977 (Bank Leu AG Zürich; Zurich, 1977).

BANK LEU

(1987): Bank Leu AG Zürich and Spink and Son Numismatics Ltd., *Asta Ceresio. Monete e medaglie.* Catalogue of Auction held on 26 September 1987 (Bank Leu AG Zürich and Spink and Son Numismatics Ltd.; Zurich, 1987).

BANTI AND SIMONETTI I

(1972): A. Banti and L. Simonetti, *Corpus Nummorum Romanorum* I (Firenze, 1973).

BELLONI

(1960): G. G. Belloni, *Le monete romane dell'età repubblicana* (Milan, 1960).

BELLONI

(1977): G. G. Belloni, *Gabinetto Numismatico* I (Milan, 1977).

BERK

(1986a): Harlan J. Berk, Ltd., *43rd Buy or Bid Sale.* Catalogue of Sale closing 28 May 1986 (Harlan J. Berk, Ltd.; Joliet, 1986).

BERK

(1986b): Harlan J. Berk, Ltd., *44th Buy or Bid Sale.* Catalogue of Sale closing 30 July 1986 (Harlan J. Berk, Ltd.; Joliet, 1986).

BERK

(1986c): Harlan J. Berk, Ltd., *45th Buy or Bid Sale.* Catalogue of Sale closing 21 October 1986 (Harlan J. Berk, Ltd.; Joliet, 1986).

BERK

(1988): Harlan J. Berk, Ltd., *55th Buy or Bid Sale.* Catalogue of Sale closing 19 October 1988) (Harlan J. Berk, Ltd.; Chicago, 1988).

BURNETT

(1977): A. M. Burnett, "The Authority to Coin in the Late Republic and Early Empire," *The Numismatic Chronicle* 1977 (Seventh Series, Volume XVII) 37–63.

BURNETT

(1978): A. M. Burnett, "The First Roman Silver Coins,"*Quaderni Ticinesi. Numismatica e Antichità Classiche* VII (1978) 121–42.

BURNETT

(1982): A. M. Burnett, "The Currency of Italy from the Hannibalic War to the Reign of Augustus," *Annali del Instituto di Numismatica* 29 (1982) 125–37.

BURNETT

(1986): A. M. Burnett, "The Iconography of Roman Coin Types in the Third Century B.C.," *The Numismatic Chronicle* 146 (1986) 66–75.

BURNETT

(1989): A. M. Burnett, "The Beginnings of Roman Coinage," *Annali. Istituto Italiana di Numismatica* 36 (1989) 33–64.

BURNETT AND CRAWFORD

(1987): A. M. Burnett and M. H. Crawford, eds., *The Coinage of the Roman World in the Late Republic* (BAR International Series 326; Oxford, 1987).

BUSSO PEUS

(1969): Dr. Busso Peus Nachf., *Katalog 271: Römer byzantiner.* Catalogue of Auction held 25 November 1969 (Dr. Busso Peus Nachf.; Frankfurt am Main, 1969).

BUTTREY

(1976): T. V. Buttrey, "The Denarii of P. Crepusius and Roman Republican Mint Organization," *American Numismatic Society Museum Notes* 21 (1976) 67–108.

BUTTREY ET AL.

(1989): T. V. Buttrey, K. T. Erim, T. D. Groves, and R. R. Holloway, *Morgantina Studies II: The Coins* (Princeton, 1989).

CALICÓ

(1983): X. and F. Calicó, *Los denarios romanos anteriores a J.C.* (Barcelona, 1983).

CAMPANA

(1987): A. Campana, *La monetazione degli insorti italici durante la Guerra Sociale (91–87 a.C.)* (Soliera, 1987).

CARSON

(1971): R. A. G. Carson, ed., *Mints, Dies and Currency* (London, 1971).

CARSON, BERGHAUS, AND LOWICK

(1979): R. Carson, P. Berghaus, and N. Lowick, eds., *A Survey of Numismatic Research 1972–1977* (International Association of Professional Numismatists Publication No. 5; Berne, 1979).

CRAWFORD

M. H. Crawford, *Roman Republican Coinage,* 2 vols. (Cambridge, 1974).

CRAWFORD

(1964): M. H. Crawford, "The Coinage of the Age of Sulla," *The Numismatic Chronicle* 1964 (Seventh Series, Volume IV) 141–58.

CRAWFORD

(1968): M. H. Crawford, "Plated Coins – False Coins," *The Numismatic Chronicle* 1968 (Seventh Series, Volume VIII) 55–59.

CRAWFORD

(1969): M. H. Crawford, *Roman Republican Coin Hoards* (Royal Numismatic Society Special Publication No. 4; London, 1969).

CRAWFORD

(1971): M. H. Crawford, "C.Censori," *The Numismatic Chronicle* 1971 (Seventh Series, Volume XI) 143–49.

CRAWFORD

(1984): M. H. Crawford, *A Catalogue of Roman Republican Coins in the Collections of the Royal Scottish Museum, Edinburgh* (Royal Scottish Museum Information Series Art and Archaeology 6; Edinburgh, 1984).

CRAWFORD

(1985): M. H. Crawford, *Coinage and Money Under the Roman Republic* (Berkeley and Los Angeles, 1985).

CURRY

(1973): M. R. Curry, "Some Aspects of Roman Plated Coins," *The Numismatic Circular* LXXXI (1973) 230–85 and 333–35.

DEPEYROT

(1985): G. Depeyrot, ed., *Les collections monnétaires I: Monnaies du monde antique* (Administration des Monnaies et Médailles; Paris, 1985).

DE RUYTER

(1996): P.H. de Ruyter, "The denarii of the Roman Republican moneyer Lucius Julius Bursio, a die analysis," *The Numismatic Chronicle* 156 (1996) 79–147.

EMPIRE COINS

(1987): Empire Coins, Inc., *Public Auction #7 of Ancient Coins.* Catalogue of Auction held 2 May 1987 (Empire Coins, Inc.; Holly Hill, 1987).

EVANS

(1987): J. D. Evans, "The Sicilian Coinage of Sextus Pompeius (Crawford 511)," *American Numismatic Society Museum Notes* 32 (1987) 97–157.

FAVA

(1969): A. S. Fava, *I simboli nelle monete argentee repubblicane e la vita dei Romani* (Museo Civico di Torino; Torino, 1969).

FORRER
(1922): L. Forrer, *The Weber Collection* I (London, 1922).

GALERIE DES MONNAIES OF GENEVA LTD.
(1978): Galerie des Monnaies of Geneva Ltd., *Greek, Roman and Byzantine Coins.* Catalogue of Auction held 9 June 1978 (Galerie des Monnaies of Geneva Ltd.; New York, 1978).

GORINI
(1973): G. Gorini, *Monete romane repubblicane del Museo Bottaci di Padova* (Venezia, 1973).

HAEBERLIN
(1910): E. J. Haeberlin, *Aes Grave. Das Schwergeld Roms und Mittelitaliens,* Text and Atlas (Frankfurt A.M., 1910).

HASSEL
(1985): E. J. Hassel, *Die münzen der römischen republik im Römisch-Germanischen Zentralmuseum (Kataloge vor- und frühgeschichtlicher altertümer* Band 24; Mainz, 1985).

HENIG
(1983): M. Henig, ed., *A Handbook of Roman Art* (Phaidon Press Limited, 1983).

HERBERT
(1987): K. Herbert, *The John Max Wulfing Collection in Washington University. Roman Republican Coins (Ancient Coins in North American Collections* No. 7; New York, 1987).

HERSH
(1976): C. A. Hersh, "A Study of the Coinage of the Moneyer C. Calpurnius Piso L. F. Frugi," *The Numismatic Chronicle* CXXXVI (Seventh Series, Volume XVI; 1976) 7–63.

HERSH
(1977): C. A. Hersh, "Notes on the Chronology and Interpretation of the Roman Republican Coinage,"*The Numismatic Chronicle* CXXXVII (Seventh Series, Volume XVII; 1977) 18–36.

HERSH AND WALKER
(1984): C. Hersh and A. Walker, "The Mesagne Hoard," *American Numismatic Society Museum Notes* 29 (1984) 103–34.

KENT
(1978): J. P. C. Kent, *Roman Coins* (London, 1978).

LANZ
(1983): Numismatik Lanz, *Auktion 26: Münzen der Antike.* Catalogue of Auction held on 5 December 1983 (Numismatik Lanz; München, 1983).

LA NIECE AND CRADDOCK
(1993): S. La Niece and P. Craddock. eds., *Metal Plating and Patination* (Boston, 1993).

LANZ
(1988): Numismatik Lanz, *Auktion 44: Münzen der Antike.* Catalogue of Auction held on 16 May 1988 (Numismatik Lanz; München, 1988).

LANZ
(1989): Numismatik Lanz, *Auktion 48: Münzen der Antike.* Catalogue of Auction held on 22 May 1989 (Numismatik Lanz; München, 1989).

LEPCZYK
(1981): Joseph Lepczyk, *Forty-third Public Auction and Mail Bid Sale for the Joint Convention of The Toronto International Coin Fair and The International Numismatic Society.* Catalogue of Auction held on 20–21 November 1981 (Joseph Lepczyk; East Lansing, 1981).

LEVY AND BASTIEN
(1985): B. E. Levy and P. C. V. Bastien, *Roman Coins in the Princeton University Library I: Republic to Commodus* (Wetteren, Belgium; 1985).

MALLOY
(l977): Alex G. Malloy, Inc., *Auction Sale X: Antiquities, Ancient Coins, Medieval Coins.* Catalogue of Mail Bid Auction closing 31 October 1977 (Alex G. Malloy, Inc.; South Salem, 1977).

MALLOY
(1978): Alex G. Malloy, Inc., *Auction Sale XII: Antiquities, Ancient Coins, Medieval Coins.* Catalogue of Mail Bid Auction closing 25 April 1978 (Alex G. Malloy, Inc.; South Salem, 1978).

MAREK
(1985): V. Marek, *Roman Republican Coins in the Collection of the Charles University* (Praha, 1985).

MARTIN
(1989): T. R. Martin, "Sulla *Imperator Iterum,* the Samnites and Roman Republican Coin Propaganda," *Scheizerische Numismatische Rundschau* 68 (1989) 19–44.

MARTINI
(1988a): R. Martini, "Note sulla distribuzione delle emissioni bronzee del DIVOS IVLIVS," *Notizie dal chiostro del Monastero Maggiore* XLI–XLII (1988) 39–42.

MARTINI
(1988b): R. Martini, "Monetazione bronzea romana tardo-repubblicana.I.," *Glaux* 1 (1988) 1–146.

MATTINGLY
(1977): H. B. Mattingly, "Coinage and the Roman State," *The Numismatic Chronicle* 1977 (Seventh Series, Volume XVII) 199–215.

MATTINGLY
(1982): H. B. Mattingly, "The Management of the Roman Republican Mint," *Annali. Instituto Italiano di Numismatica* 29 (1982) 9–46.

METCALF
(1976): W. E. Metcalf, review of *Roman Republican Coinage* by M. H. Crawford, *American Journal of Archaeology* 80 (1976) 215–16.

MORAWIECKI
(1983): L. Morawiecki, *Political Propaganda in the Coinage of the Late Republic (44–43 B.C.)* (Wroclaw, 1983).

MÜNZEN UND MEDAILLEN
(1958): Münzen und Medaillen A.G., *Liste 175* (January 1958) (Münzen und Medaillen A.G.; Basel, 1958).

MÜNZEN UND MEDAILLEN
(1970): Münzen und Medaillen A.G., *Vente publique 43.* Catalogue of Auction held on 12 and 13 November 1970 (Münzen und Medaillen A.G.; Basel, 1970).

MÜNZEN UND MEDAILLEN
(1973): Münzen und Medaillen A.G., *Liste 344* (April 1973) (Münzen und Medaillen A.G.; Basel, 1973).

MÜNZEN UND MEDAILLEN
(1975): Münzen und Medaillen A.G., *Vente publique 52.* Catalogue of Auction held on 19 and 20 June 1975 (Münzen und Medaillen A.G.; Basel, 1975).

MÜNZEN UND MEDAILLEN
(1982): Münzen und Medaillen A.G., *Vente publique 61.* Catalogue of Auction held on 7 and 8 October 1982 (Münzen und Medaillen A.G.; Basel, 1982).

MÜNZEN UND MEDAILLEN
(1984): Münzen und Medaillen A.G., *Vente publique 66.* Catalogue of Auction held on 22 and 23 October 1984 (Münzen und Medaillen A.G.; Basel, 1984).

MÜNZEN UND MEDAILLEN
(1986): Münzen und Medaillen A.G., *Liste 490* (July 1986) (Münzen und Medaillen A.G.; Basel, 1986).

MÜNZEN UND MEDAILLEN
(1989): Münzen und Medaillen A.G., *Liste 524* (August 1989) (Münzen und Medaillen A.G.; Basel, 1989).

NFA
(1979): Numismatic Fine Arts, Inc., *Auction VI: Ancient Coins.* Catalogue of Auction held on 27–28 February 1979 (Numismatic Fine Arts, Inc.; Beverly Hills, 1979).

NFA
(1981): Numismatic Fine Arts, Inc., *Auction X: Ancient Coins.* Catalogue of Auction held on 17–18 September 1981 (Numismatic Fine Arts, Inc.; Beverly Hills, 1981).

NS
(1977): The Numismatic Studio, *Ancient Roman and Greek; Coins of the World; Gold and Silver* (The Numismatic Studio; Bayside, Fall, 1977).

NAVILLE IV
Naville & Cie, *Monnaies Grecques Antiques.* Catalogue of Auction held on 16 June 1922 (Naville & Cie; Geneva, 1922).

NAVILLE X
Naville & Cie, *Monnaies Grecques et Romaines.* Catalogue of Auction held on 15–18 June 1925 (Naville & Cie; Geneva, 1925).

NIGGELER
(1966): Bank Leu & Co. AG and Münzen und Medaillen AG, *Sammlung Walter Niggeler 2 Teil.* Catalogue of Auction held on 21 and 22 October 1966 (Bank Leu & Co. AG and Münzen und Medaillen AG; Basel, 1966).

OWL LTD. AND MCKENNA
(1980): Owl Ltd. and Thomas P. McKenna, *The Aurelia Collection of Roman Republican Silver Coins* (Owl Ltd. and Thomas P. McKenna; Fort Collins, 1980).

PANVINI ROSATI
(1966): F. Panvini Rosati, *La moneta di Roma repubblicana* (Bologna, 1966).

RATTO
(1927): Rudolfo Ratto, *Monnaies grecques.* Catalogue of Auction beginning on 4 April 1927 (Rudolfo Ratto; Lugano, 1926).

RATTO
(1928): Rudolfo Ratto: *Monnaies grecques. Monnaies romaines.* Catalogue of Auction starting 8 February 1928 (Rudolfo Ratto; Lugano, 1927).

SCHULMAN
(1966): Jacques Schulman N.V., *The Richard J. Graham Collection of Ancient Greek, Roman and Byzantine Coins.* Catalogue 243 of Auction held on 8 to 10 June 1966 (Jacques Schulman N.V.; Amsterdam, 1966).

SCHULMAN
(1974): Jacques Schulman B.V., *Coins and Medals including Roman and Byzantine Coins.* Catalogue 258 of Auction held on 10 to 13 June 1974 (Jacques Schulman B.V.; Amsterdam, 1974).

SCHULMAN
(1981): Jacques Schulman B.V., *Fixed Price-list of Archaeology and Ancient Coins* 220 (Jacques Schulman B.V.; Amsterdam, May 1981).

SNG COPENHAGEN
(1942): *Sylloge Nummorum Graecorum, The Royal Collection of Coins and Medals.* Danish National Museum, *Italy* vol. I, fasc. 1 (1942).

SOTHEBY
(1908): Sotheby, Wilkinson and Hodge, *The O'Hagan Coin Collection. Catalogue of the Collection of Roman Coins in Gold, Silver and Bronze, formed by H. Osborne O'Hagan, Esq..* Catalogue of Auction held on 13–17 and 20–22 July 1908 (Sotheby, Wilkinson and Hodge; London, 1908).

SOTHEBY
(1983): Sotheby Parke Bernet & Co. A.G., *The Brand Collection [Part 3]: Greek and Roman Coins.* Catalogue of Auction held on 9 June 1983 (Sotheby Parke Bernet & Co. A.G.; Zurich, 1983).

SPINK AND SON LTD.
(1977): Spink and Son Ltd., *The Numismatic Circular* LXXXV (Spink and Son Ltd.; London, 1977).

SUKIENNIK
(1985): G. Sukiennik, *Catalogue of Ancient Coins in the Ossoliński National Institute Library* Part 1 (Wroclaw, 1985).

SUPERIOR
(1988): Superior Stamp and Coin Co., Inc., *The Moreira Collection Sale, Part 1.* Catalogue of Auction held on 31 May and 1 June 1988 (Superior Stamp and Coin Co., Inc.; Beverly Hills, 1988).

SYDENHAM:
E. A. Sydenham, *The Coinage of the Roman Republic* (London, 1952).

SYDENHAM
(1926): E. A. Sydenham, *Aes Grave* (London, 1926).

THOMSEN
(1961): R. Thomsen, *Early Roman Coinage* I–III (Copenhagen, 1957–1961).

THURLOW AND VECCHI
(1979): B. Thurlow and I. G. Vecchi, *Italian Cast Coinage and Italian Aes Rude, Signatum and the Aes Grave of Sicily* (Dorchester, 1979).

WHITEHEAD
(1975): D. H. E. Whitehead, *Roman Coins in the McGill University Collection* (M. Woloch, ed., *The McGill University Collection of Greek and Roman Coins I* (Amsterdam, 1975).

NOTES AND CONVENTIONS

The entries have been arranged chronologically, following Crawford, and within each issue, the coins are arranged by weight or by the alphabetic or numerical progression of control marks. No attempt has been made to do exhaustive die-linkages but those that have turned up in the course of study have been recorded. Plated coins have been listed under their respective Crawford number for future studies of their dies (for their illegality, see Crawford [1968]). None have iron cores (see La Niece and Craddock [1993] 223–46). Specific gravities have been given for coins which have suspiciously low weights or are low in weight when compared with others from the same issues in the collection. Punchmarks, made to see if a coin was plated, are mentioned where they are present. *Aes rude* are listed under Appendix A, other Italic cast bronze coins under Appendix B, and issues from the Social War (91–87 BC) are given under Appendix C.

Each catalogue entry gives the accession number, the die-axis as on a clock-face, the weight, comments on the obverse and reverse, and the former collection or sale where known. The photographs are reproduced at 1:1. The following abbreviations have been used:

obv. = obverse

rev. = reverse

r. = right

l. = left

g = gram

mm = millimetre

s.g. = specific gravity

publ. = published

acc. = accession

no./s. = number/s

var. = variant

INTRODUCTION

The collection of Roman Republican coins in the Royal Ontario Museum is the largest in a Canadian institution. The Republican coins in the McGill University Collection, Montreal, were published in 1975, see Whitehead (1975) 1–5, while the National Currency Collection at the Bank of Canada, Ottawa, McMaster University, Hamilton, and the Nickle Arts Museum, Calgary, also have Republican holdings.

The present catalogue lists all Roman Republican coins in the Royal Ontario Museum, as well as certain issues of the Imperatorial period in the collection not listed in Crawford, specimens of *Aes Rude* (see Appendix A), Italic cast bronze issues (see Appendix B) and issues from the Social War of 91–87 BC (see Appendix C). Unidentifiable coins have been excluded.

In total, 534 pieces of bronze and coins are published in this volume. Until 1949, coins were not listed in the original museum inventories and it has sometimes been necessary to reconstruct probable sources from dealers' tickets that remained with a coin by chance, listings on dealers' invoices, or letters from such sources as the late J. G. Milne of the Ashmolean Museum. Mr. Milne was keenly interested in the Royal Ontario Museum through his long association with C. T. Currelly, the first Director of the Royal Ontario Museum of Archaeology, one of the five museums that later formed the ROM. Mr. Milne kept abreast of the growth of the museum's numismatic collections and would acquire coins to fill gaps in the collections when he visited dealers in London and elsewhere.

The earliest acquisitions (Acc. No. 908.55.-) of Roman Republican coins were obtained by Mr. Milne from Sotheby, Wilkinson and Hodge's auction in 1908 of the Roman coins collected by H. Osborne O'Hagan. Mr. Milne acquired lots containing several coins, but when similar coins later came into the ROM collection with the same Babelon (1885) designation, it has often not been possible to determine which were originally from the O'Hagan Collection. Mr. Milne purchased another group of 65 coins (Acc. No. 921.62.-) for the museum in March 1921, but very few records remain of where he had obtained them.

The series with the accession number 912x17.- was arbitrarily assigned that number probably in the early 1950s and the author has been unable to determine why, although the "x"should indicate a belief at the time that the group had come into the ROM in or prior to 1912. The "x" designation was also used for coins numbered 948x171.-, 949x15.-, and 950x24.-.

One Republican bronze coin (Acc. No. 921.6.12) was in a collection given to the ROM by a Mrs. Travers in 1921 and three were among a large collection donated by G. A. Farini in 1923 (Acc. No. 923.45.-). Four silver and bronze coins were in the McCaul collection (Acc. No. 924.3.-) given by the University of Toronto in 1924. In 1934, the only gold coin in the collection (No. 486) was given by the Members of the Royal Ontario Museum. In 1950, A. E. Ames gave a sum of money to the museum for coins and a large number of Roman Republican coins already in the collection were designated as The A. E. Ames Collection (Acc. No. 950.56.-).

The author began sorting the museum's Republican coins in 1969 and all coins without sources were assigned at that time to a 969x134.- accession series. One denarius was among a donation of coins by J. Beres in 1973 (Acc. No. 973.296.-). The latest additions to the collection were given in 1987 and 1989 by R. Cryderman (Acc. Nos. 987.257.- and 989.296.2), in 1989 by R. E. Hindley (Acc. No. 989.117.1), and in 1991 by Dr. and Mrs. A. D. Tushingham (Acc. No. 991.219.35).

Since no attempt appears to have been made to have the collection reflect the entire history of Roman Republican coinage, some periods are better represented than others such as the Imperatorial coinage.

Athough the Greek colonies in southern Italy began issuing silver coins about 530 BC, central Italy still used bronze as its metal medium of exchange because the necessary ores were readily available in the area. The bronze was not formed into coins but rather into chunks of bullion. The earliest specimens in the ROM's collection are listed under Appendix A: the two pieces of bronze *aes rude* (A1 and 2) used as a medium of exchange in central Italy for many centuries and still appearing in such third century BC hoards in Italy as Crawford (1969) 44.8 (Cerveteri before 1885), 44.10 (Vulci 1828), 45.13 (Ariccia 1848), 46.20 (Ardea 1940), and 63.81 (Via Tiberina 1941). All of these hoards contained *aes rude* as well as later cast ingots and/or coins.

After Rome extended its control over central Italy, it began to be drawn into the affairs of southern Italy, culminating in the Pyrrhic War in which Pyrrhus, king of Epiros, went to war against the Romans on behalf of the city of Tarentum in 280 BC and was finally defeated in 275 BC.

Various places in central Italy began to cast bronze bullion in the form of bars or ingots, some bearing a raised design. In the catalogue, No. 1 is the only fragment in the collection that illustrates the cast bronze bars of Rome. Ten major varieties of these with designs in relief on both sides have been assigned to Rome and dated to the period of the Pyrrhic War down to about 260 BC (see Crawford, 41-2.n.5 and 716–18). They would appear to have been a form of bullion that could easily be divided into measured amounts.

When Rome began to strike her earliest silver coins, she was influenced by the coins being issued by the Greek cities to the south (see Burnett [1989] 55–57). The unit used was the didrachm or two-drachma coin (for the suggestion that these were actually tridrachms, see Burnett [1989] 34.n.10), and four successive types were struck. The earliest, dating to about 310–300 BC, has the helmeted head of Mars on the obverse and a horse's head with ROMANO on the reverse (No. 2).

Along with the didrachms, Rome began issuing successive series of large cast bronze coins in units based on the as or Roman pound (see Crawford 590–92) (Nos. 3–22); for a different view of the dating of the didrachms and associated bronze issues, see Mattingly [1977] 199–203. (For a discussion of the iconography of the helmeted head of Roma and the influence of Alexander the Great on the early designs used by the Romans, see Burnett [1986].) Counterparts of the cast bronze coins in other areas of central Italy are included under Appendix B.

In 225–217 BC, Rome began issuing cast bronze denominations with the head of a different god on the obverse of each denomination and a prow on the reverse, and marked with their value (Nos. 26–34, based on an as weighing about 268 g). These types henceforth were generally used whenever bronze denominations were issued. At the same time, didrachms (No. 24) were introduced with the janiform head of the Dioscuri on the obverse and Jupiter in a quadriga on the reverse. These later became very debased (No. 25).

The next developments were the use of the semilibral as at about half the previous weight and the introduction of striking instead of casting for the denominations from the sextans to quartuncia (Nos. 35–46). The higher denominations were cast as before.

After 215 BC, the weights of the post semilibral bronze denominations were dropping (Nos. 47–50) and certain issues were marked by their mints, such as Sicily (No. 51) and Luceria (No. 52).

About 211 BC, a new group of silver issues was introduced: the victoriatus (Nos. 53–54), three gold denominations, the denarius (No. 55), the quinarius (No. 56), and the sestertius (No. 57). The types or designs used for the victoriatus were the head of Jupiter and Victory crowning a trophy. The original types used for the denarius and the remaining silver issues were the helmeted head of Roma on the obverse and the Dioscuri on horseback on the reverse. The earliest issues of the new denominations were anonymous, but letters or symbols indicating the issuing mints or moneyers were later added (Nos. 64–75).

The denarius, originally worth 10 asses and retariffed about 141 BC at 16 asses, was to remain the chief denomination until AD 214 when the Emperor Caracalla introduced the double denarius or antoninianus which gradually replaced the denarius.

Starting with issues dating to 209–208 BC, all the bronze denominations were struck. (For the reduction in weight of the bronze denominations, see Crawford 595–97.) The ROM collection has no bronze coins from 127 BC (No. 151) until 45 BC (No. 494) and, indeed, none was struck from 82 to 46–45 BC.

The reverse of the denarius later bore the figure of Luna in a biga (No. 75) as well as the Dioscuri (No. 78), and later the figure of Victory in a biga (Nos. 83–84) was also introduced. Most of the issues were now signed with an abbreviation of the name of the moneyer responsible.

In the ROM's collection, the widening of the choice of the representation for the reverse is first seen on Nos. 115–16, where the goddess Juno is driving a biga of goats on denarii struck by C. Renius in 138 BC, while the earliest appearance of a substitute for the head of Roma on the obverse is the head of Mars on a denarius struck by Ti. Veturius (No. 120) in the following year. The reverse of this coin, an oath-taking scene, is political, showing the moneyer's support of the ratification in 137 of the *foedus Numantinum*. The passing of the Lex Gabinia in 139, which allowed secret ballots in elections, encouraged the use of coin types as self-advertisement by the moneyers and their families. The reverse type of Nos. 131–32, showing the Columna Minucia, is a reminder of the monument erected to L. Minucius, an ancestor of the moneyer Ti. Minucius C.f. Augurinus, in connection with a grain distribution in 439 BC.

From the issue by C. Cato in 123 BC (No. 165) to those of M. Calidius, Q. Metellus and Cn. Fulvius in 117–116 BC (Nos. 185–87), the representations used on coins struck at Rome are without any personal themes or symbols and usually include only the moneyers' names. After this, personal types are again to be found.

Political backing of an unrelated influential Roman can be seen in the references to Gaius Marius, who won the first of his consulships in 107 BC, on coins issued by the moneyer C. Fundanius. On the reverse of a denarius (No. 258), the *triumphator* in a quadriga probably represents Marius himself. On the reverse of the quinarii (Nos. 259–60), the figure of Victory crowning a trophy accompanied by a Gaulish *carnyx* or trumpet and a captive refers to the victories of Marius over the Teutones and Cimbri.

When the Italic allies revolted in the Social or Marsian War of 91–87 BC, they struck their own denarii, three of which are included in Appendix C. Both Marius and his rival, Lucius Cornelius Sulla, played a part in the Social War and afterwards, with the death of Marius in 86 BC, Sulla's influence was supreme.

No. 336 was struck in the name of Sulla in 84–83 BC with Venus, his family's patron deity, on the obverse and trophies, representing his military achievements, on the reverse. Symbols of Sulla's victories as well as personal types occur on the issues of the moneyers prior to Sulla's retirement in 79 BC.

Some of the events that occurred in the years between Sulla's retirement and the rise of Pompey are reflected in the representations on the Republic's coins. Issued in 76–75 BC, Nos. 377–788 depict the Genius populi Romani on the obverse and the sceptre and wreath with the globe and rudder. These refer to the need of the Roman people to dominate over the land and sea, therefore backing the subjugation of the general Sertorius who was controlling most of Spain.

The power of Pompey in the affairs of Rome is seen in No. 428, issued in 56 BC by Faustus Cornelius Sulla, Sulla's son, where the large wreath is the *corona aurea* granted to Pompey in 63 BC and the three smaller wreaths signify his triumphs.

Opposition to the possible granting of a dictatorship to Pompey can be seen in the two denarii (Nos. 443–44) issued by M. Iunius Brutus in 54 BC. The head of Libertas is on the obverse of the first and on its reverse, Brutus'ancestor L. Iunius Brutus, the founder of the Roman Republic. On the second, the head of L. Iunius Brutus is paired with the head of another ancestor, C. Servilius Ahala, who allegedly saved Rome by murdering Spurius Maelius, suspected of being a prospective tyrant.

Personal types chosen by the moneyer continued to appear, such as No. 445 with which C. Coelius Caldus honoured C. Coelius Caldus who was Consul in 94 BC. The latter's portrait appears on the obverse with a tablet referring to the Lex Coelia Tabellaria, passed when he was Tribune in 107 BC. The oval shield on the reverse alludes to his defeat of the Salluvii in Gaul and the head of Sol and the Macedonian shield to a successful military action in the East.

The achievements of Julius Caesar began to be seen in the coinage with the issuing in 49–48 BC of Nos. 447–48. The priestly implements on the obverse recall his election as Pontifex Maximus in 63 BC. On his second issue (Nos. 461–62), struck from 13 July 48 to 47 BC, Caesar's fifty-second birthday is marked by the numerals behind the female head, while the trophy and Gallic shield refer to his victories over the Gauls and the axe to his position of

Pontifex Maximus.

The only aureus in the collection (No. 486) was issued in 46 BC for Caesar by the Praetor Aulus Hirtius, who later became Consul in 43 BC. Both sides of the coin refer to Caesar as Pontifex Maximus: the veiled female head portrays the hearth-goddess Vesta, whose rites were under the control of the Pontifex Maximus, and the axe and jug signifies the office of the Pontifex and the curved staff, the augurate.

The interests of the Pompeian faction continued outside Rome after Pompey's murder in 48 BC. Nos. 491–92 were struck by loyalists under Pompey's sons in Spain during 46 to 45 BC. The helmeted head of Roma is on the obverse and, on the reverse, a Pompeian soldier, standing on the prow of a ship, is being welcomed by a woman with a palm branch. A commemorative portrait of Pompey appears on No. 495 in the guise of Janus, struck in Spain and Sicily in 45 BC onwards, and on No. 506, struck in Sicily in 42 to 40 BC.

After the assassination of Caesar on the Ides of March in 44 BC, a struggle began both for the leadership of the Caesarians and against the murderers of Caesar. (For an examination of the propaganda on coins of 44 to 43 BC, see Morawiecki [1983]). In 43 BC, M. Antonius, M. Lepidus (Consul with Caesar in 46 BC) and Octavian (Caesar's grand-nephew and heir) finally agreed to form the Second Triumvirate. The anti-Caesarians were finally defeated at the battle of Philippi in 42 BC. No. 507 was struck in 41 BC by M. Barbatius for Antonius with the portrait of Antonius on the obverse and that of Octavian on the reverse.

The first portrait of Caesar on coins had appeared shortly before his death but the earliest in the collection is No. 508, struck in 40 BC or later. Q. Voconius Vitulus placed a posthumous portrait of Caesar on the obverse and on the reverse, a calf or *vitulus*. On No. 510, Octavian associated himself with the deified Caesar by using both their portraits on a bronze issue of around 38 BC.

As part of the reconciliation at Brundisium in 40 BC between M. Antonius and Octavian, M. Antonius married Octavia, Octavian's sister, and on Nos. 514–15 their portraits appear on the obverse of asses issued by M. Oppius Capito.

The last coins in the catalogue (Nos. 516–24) are representative of the large legionary issues of M. Antonius, struck during his military preparations which culminated in the Battle of Actium in 31 BC when he and Cleopatra were finally defeated by Octavian.

For a description of the early developments in Roman coinage and a full account of previous research on the subject, see Thomsen (1961), with additional information up to 1971 in Crawford (for an extensive review of Crawford, see Mattingly [1977]), as well as Crawford (1985) 1–51. The major English publication on Roman Republican coinage by E. A. Sydenham in 1952 has been superceded by Crawford and the chronology given in the latter work has been followed in this catalogue. Discussions of individual moneyers and explanations about the types they chose to use on their coins are included in Crawford, as is information on the technology, weight standards, administration and other facets of Roman Republican coinage, together with an extensive bibliography. The dating of the issues is not necessarily certain, as is evidenced by other authorities referred to in the catalogue.

With the exception of the *aes rude* (Appendix A), the Italic cast coins (Appendix B), the issues of the Social War (Appendix C), and Nos. 514–15, struck for M. Antonius, all the issues published in this catalogue were included in Crawford. The coins used in the various Roman provinces during the later Republic are described in Crawford (1985) and Burnett and Crawford (1987) and an overview of the currency of Italy during the last two centuries of the Republic is given in Burnett (1982).

The administration of the production of Republican coinage throughout its history is not straightforward but see Mattingly (1982) 9ff. The earliest occurrence of a moneyer's actual name in the ROM's collection is on No. 76, struck in 179–170 BC, although earlier moneyers are recorded in other collections.

Colleges of three moneyers, men who were at the beginning of their political careers and were either elected (see Crawford 602–3) or appointed (see Burnett [1977] 37–44), are evident in the conjunction of the names on such coins as No. 184 with the initials Q.MAR, C.F, and L.R, and Nos. 185–87, issued by M.CALID, Q.MET, and CN.FOVL. The earliest appearance in the collection of the actual title for the college of moneyers—*tresviri aere argento auro flando feriundo*—is the abbreviation III.VIR on No. 391 after the name GETA on the obverse. Caesar later increased the number of moneyers from three to four.

Issues also occur in which the designation of a magistracy is given, indicating that they were not struck by a moneyer but by the magistrate designated in the legend. The earliest recorded instance is the abbreviation Q for Quaestor after M. Sergius Silus' name on his issue of 116–115 BC at Rome (Nos. 192–96). The Quaestors were in charge of the moneyers. This practice continued to occur sporadically on later issues.

Other magistrates represented in the collection are M. Fannius and L. Critonius as Plebeian Aediles in 86 BC on No. 321, with both obverse and reverse referring to their responsibilities for the grain supply, and P. Furius Crassipes as Curule Aedile in 84 BC on No. 332, with the curule seat on the reverse.

In addition to the issues struck by the moneyers in Rome on behalf of the Senate during the first century BC, independent military issues were struck outside Rome in the name of such commanders as Sulla (No. 336), Caesar (Nos. 447–48, 461–62, 467–69, 489–90), Pompey's son Cnaeus (Nos. 491–92, 506), and, after Caesar's assassination, M. Antonius (Nos. 507, 514–15, 516–24) and Octavian (No. 513).

A number of denarii with serrated edges are in the collection, the earliest being No. 67, dating from 209–208 BC, and latest, Nos. 404–5 from 64 BC. Why certain issues were struck on flans that were serrated before striking is unclear (see Crawford 581). If the practice was to guard against plated forgeries, it was unsuccessful since No. 183 is a plated denarius with a serrated edge within a group of genuine denarii serrati (Nos. 180–82) from the same moneyers. The issues of L.PROCILI F, struck in 80 BC, have both types of edges: Nos. 355–57 are unserrated while No. 359, from his other issue, is serrated.

The technical competency of the engravers who produced the dies for the coins of the Roman Republican period varied greatly, as can be seen in the crude head of Roma on No. 164 compared with those on Nos. 157 to 163, all issued by Q. Fabius Labeo in 124 BC. Later, among the issues of Caesar, the rendering of the features of the goddess on Nos. 461–62 is harsh in comparision to the naturalistic depiction of Venus on Nos. 467–69.

Although the goddess Roma always wears her helmet and jewellery, variations in her depiction can include showing her as matronly and slightly plump, as on Nos. 128–29, or as a delicately featured young woman, as on No. 197. The die-engravers, whose names are unknown to us, do not appear to have had a strict set of standards concerning workmanship or style. (For the more obvious use of the drill in the second half of the first century BC, see Henig [1983] 168.)

In addition to the coins listed in this catalogue, the ROM collection includes the following modern forgeries: Crawford 14/3, 24/5, 43/1, 238/1, 245/1, 270/1, 343/2b, 349/1, 374/2, 379/1a, 407/1, 407/2, 410/5, 410/6, 412/1, 427/1, 428/2, 429/2a (two copies of the same coin), 432/1 (two copies of the same coin), 440/1, 443/1, 489/3, and a hybrid with the obverse of 407/1 and the reverse of 443/1.

THE CATALOGUE

ANONYMOUS   Mint: Rome. 260–242 BC
Bronze ingot. Trident tied with fillet/caduceus tied with fillet. Crawford 11/1.
1.   921.62.59 121.41 g. Length, 44.3 mm; width, 28.1 mm; height, 17.9 mm. Found at Chiusi. Ex Weber Collection, Forrer (1922) no. 115. Although very little remains, the surviving relief-decoration and its position in relation to the lower corner of the ingot are reminiscent of such trident/caduceus ingots as Haeberlin (1910) taf. 41.2–3.

ANONYMOUS   Mint: Metapontum? 280–276 BC (not Metapontum but an uncertain mint, about 310–300 BC, Crawford [1985] 29)
Didrachm. Obv.: bearded head of Mars l.; behind, oak-spray. Rev.: horse's head r. on base; behind, ear of grain; on base, ROMANO. Crawford 13/1.
2.   925.2.92 7 7.32 g. From same dies as Burnett (1978) pl. 1.9 (obv. die Ob and rev. die R7) and Münzen und Medaillen (1958) 2.31.

ANONYMOUS   Mint: Rome. 280–276 BC
Semis (cast). Obv.: head of Minerva l.; below, ⌣. Rev.: female head l.; below, ⌣. Crawford 14/2.
3.   912x17.21 1 161.85 g.
4.   912x17.3 11 157.86 g.

Triens (cast). Obv.: thunderbolt; on l., ·· ; on r., ·· . Rev.: dolphin r.; below, ···· . Crawford 14/3.
5.   912x17.6 115 g.
6.   969x134.183 95.90 g.
7.   969x134.184 88.71 g. Rev.: many air holes.

Quadrans (cast). Obv.: r. hand; on l., ⁝ . Rev.: two barley grains; between, ⁝ . Crawford 14/4.
8.   912x17.9 77.40 g. From the same mould as Haeberlin (1910) taf. 40.5.
9.   912x17.8 75.29 g.

ANONYMOUS   Mint: Rome. Shortly before 269 BC (Cosa, after 264 BC, Crawford [1985] 38–39)
Litra (struck) (half-obol, Crawford [1984] 1.2). Obv.: head of Minerva (Roma, see Burnett [1989] 38) l. Rev.: horse's head r. on base; behind, ROMANO upwards. Crawford 17/1a.
10.   948x171.6 3 5.60 g.
11.   949x15.834 3 4.72 g. Obv.: gryphon on helmet.

ANONYMOUS   Mint: Rome. 275–270 BC
Semis (cast). Obv.: Pegasus r.; below, S. Rev.: Pegasus l.; below, S. Crawford 18/2.
12.   912x17.4 12 155.09 g. Rev.: retouched.

Triens (cast). Obv.: horse's head r.; below, ···· . Rev.: horse's head l.; below, ···· . Crawford 18/3.
13.   912x17.7 12 103.39 g.

Quadrans (cast). Obv.: boar r.; below, ··· . Rev.: boar l.; below, ··· . Crawford 18/4.
14.   912x17.10 12 82.84 g.
15.   969x134.99 12 76.40 g.

Sextans (cast). Obv.: head of one of the Dioscuri r.; behind, : . Rev.: head of one of the Dioscuri l.; behind, : . Crawford 18/5.
16.   912x17.11 12 55.88 g.

ANONYMOUS   Mint: Rome. 269–266 BC
Sextans (cast). Obv.: exterior of scallop-shell; below, ·· . Rev.: interior of scallop-shell. Crawford 21/5.
17.   912x17.14 12 42.23 g.

Uncia (cast). Obv.: knucklebone seen from outside. Rev.: knucklebone seen from inside. Crawford 21/6.
18.   925.2.67 12 21.00 g. Obv.: without mark of value. Naville X lot 1643.

ANONYMOUS   Mint: Rome. 265–242 BC
Quadrans (cast). Obv.: dog l.; in exergue, ··· . Rev.: six-spoked wheel with ··· in three adjacent interstices. Crawford 24/6a.
19.   969x134.63 64.55 g.

Sextans (cast). Obv.: tortoise. Rev.: six-spoked wheel; ·· between two spokes. Crawford 24/7.
20.   912x17.15 43.67 g. Rev.: without mark of value.

ANONYMOUS   Mint: Rome. 241–235 BC
As (cast). Obv.: janiform head of the Dioscuri. Rev.: head of Mercury l.; behind, sickle. Crawford 25/4.
21.   912x17.12 12 280.27 g.

Triens (cast). Obv.: thunderbolt; on l., ·· ; on r., ·· . Rev.: dolphin r.; above, sickle; below, ···· . Crawford 25/6.
22.   912x17.13 85.87 g.

ANONYMOUS   Mint: Rome. 234–231 BC
Half-litra (struck). Obv.: head of Roma r. Rev.: dog r.; in exergue, ROMA . Crawford 26/4.
23.   948x171.7 6 2.34 g.

ANONYMOUS   Mint: Rome. 225–212 BC
Didrachm. Obv.: janiform head of Dioscuri. Rev.: Jupiter in quadriga r., driven by Victory; incuse on tablet, ROMA . Crawford 28/3.
24.   989.117.1 5.5 6.56 g. No. 24 would appear to belong to the third group connected with Crawford's mainstream sequence as Crawford pl. III.4. Ex *NFA, Fall Mail Bid Sale* (Oct. 12, 1988), no.615.
25.   924.3.189 8 2.81 g (s.g. 6.229). Debased and extremely worn, cf. Crawford 553.125, and may not be Crawford 28/3.

ANONYMOUS   Mint: Rome. 225–217 BC
As (cast). Obv.: head of Janus; below, − . Rev.: prow r.; above, I . Crawford 35/1.
26.   921.62.58 12 263.55 g. Ex Weber Collection (Siena, 1881), Forrer (1922) no. 125. Publ.: Haeberlin (1910) 32.713.
27.   912x17.17 12 248.40 g.

Semis (cast). Obv.: head of Saturn l.; below, ∽ . Rev.: prow r.; above, S . Crawford 35/2.
   28. 921.62.62 12 141.04 g. Ex Weber Collection, Forrer (1922) no. 126.
      Publ.: Haeberlin (1910) 39.63.
   29. 912x17.22 12 116.70 g.
   30. 912x17.20 12 110.74 g.

Triens (cast). Obv.: head of Minerva l.; below, ···· . Rev.: prow r.; below, ···· . Crawford 35/3a.
   31. 921.62.63 12 87.74 g. Ex Weber Collection (Dr. Diruf, 1882), Forrer (1922) no. 128.
      Publ.: Haeberlin (1910) 43.232.

Quadrans (cast). Obv.: head of Hercules l.; behind, ⋮ . Rev.: prow r.; below, ··· . Crawford 35/4.
   32. 921.62.64 12 71.90 g. Ex Weber Collection (Dr. Diruf, 1882), Forrer (1922) no. 129.
      Publ.: Haeberlin (1910) 45.40.

Sextans (cast). Obv.: head of Mercury l.; below, ·· . Rev.: prow r.; below, ·· . Crawford 35/5.
   33. 912x17.23 1 44.85 g.

Uncia (cast). Obv.: head of Roma l.; behind, · . Rev.: prow r.; below, · . Crawford 35/6.
   34. 921.62.65 12 21.31 g. Recorded as ex Weber Collection but does not match Haeberlin (1910) 50.74 or Forrer (1922) no. 131.

ANONYMOUS (semilibral) Mint: Rome. 217–215 BC
   Sextans (struck). Obv.: head of Mercury r.; above, ·· . Rev.: prow r.; above, ROMΛ ; below, ·· . Crawford 38/5.
   35. 912x17.25 1 30.34 g. Obv.: from same die as Haeberlin (1910) taf. 45.15.

Uncia (struck). Obv.: head of Roma l.; behind, · . Rev.: prow r.; above, ROMA ; below, · . Crawford 38/6.
   36. 987.257.36 8 12.75 g. Gift of R. Cryderman.
   37. 969x134.168 9 11.05 g. Rev.: ROMΛ.
   38. 912x17.26 5 10.58 g.
   39. 969x134.180 2 10.17 g.

Semuncia (struck). Obv.: head of Mercury r. Rev.: prow r.; above, ROMΛ . Crawford 38/7.
   40. 912x17.28 11 6.08 g.
   41. 969x134.170 5 5.65 g.
   42. 923.45.69 1 5.57 g. Not illustrated.
   43. 969x134.169 1 5.39 g.
   44. 912x17.27 11 5.04 g. Rev.: ROMA .

Quartuncia (struck). Obv.: head of Roma r. Rev.: prow r.; above, ROMΛ . Crawford 38/8.
   45. 912x17.29 6 3.06 g.

ANONYMOUS (semilibral) Mint: Rome. 217–215 BC
   Uncia (struck). Obv.: draped bust of Sol, facing; on l., · . Rev.: crescent; above, · between two stars; below, ROMΛ. Crawford 39/4.
   46. 969x134.175 5 8.64 g.

ANONYMOUS (post-semilibral) Mint: Rome. 215–212 BC
   As (cast). Obv.: head of Janus. Rev.: prow l., above, I . Crawford 41/5a.
   47. 969x134.167 12 109.19 g.
   48. 912x17.30 12 73.43 g.
   49. 912x17.31 1 64.92 g.

As (cast). Obv.: head of Janus. Rev.: prow r.; above, I . Crawford 41/5b.
   50. 969x134.187 11 65.49 g.

GRAIN-EAR Mint: Sicily. 214–212 BC
   Uncia (struck). Obv.: head of Roma r.; behind, · . Rev.: prow r.; above, grain-ear and ROMA ; below, · . Crawford 42/4.
   51. 969x134.190 1.5 5.22 g. Rev.: the grain-ear is unclear.

Ꞁ Mint: Luceria. 214–212 BC
   Sextans (struck). Obv.: head of Mercury r.; above, ·· . Rev.: prow r.; above, ROMΛ ; below, Ꞁ . Crawford 43/4.
   52. 969x134.171 3 10.02 g.

ANONYMOUS Mint: Rome. After 211 BC
   Victoriatus. Obv.: head of Jupiter r. Rev.: Victory r., crowning trophy; in exergue, ROMA . Crawford 44/1.
   53. 969x134.123 12 2.68 g.
   54. 969x134.122 3 2.65 g.

Denarius. Obv.: head of Roma r.; behind, X . Rev.: Dioscuri on horseback r.; below, ROMA in linear frame. Crawford 44/5; see Metcalf (1976) 215 for his disagreement on the simultaneous striking of Crawford 44/5 and 53/2 at Rome.
   55. 950.56.94 10 4.02 g.

Quinarius. Obv.: head of Roma r.; behind, V . Rev.: Dioscuri as above; below, ROMA in linear frame. Crawford 44/6.
   56. 969x134.9 1.5 1.35 g (s.g. 10.244). Broken. Rev.: ROMΛ.

Sestertius. Obv.: head of Roma r.; behind, IIS . Rev.: Dioscuri as above; below, ROMΛ in linear frame. Crawford 44/7.
   57. 950x24.1 9 0.94 g. Obv.: hair in loose waves as Crawford pl. IX.19.

ANONYMOUS Mint: Rome. After 211 BC but not among the very earliest groups, see Carson, Berghaus and Lowick (1979) 171.
   Victoriatus. Obv.: head of Jupiter r. Rev.: Victory r., crowning trophy; in exergue, ROMA . Crawford 53/1.
   58. 969x134.124 10 2.86 g.
   59. 950.56.93 3 2.63 g. Obv.: from a die by the same engraver as No. 76.
   60. 912x17.36 10 1.61 g. Plated.

Denarius. Obv.: head of Roma r.; behind, X. Rev.: Dioscuri on horseback r.; in exergue, ROMΛ in linear frame. Crawford 53/2.
   61. 950.56.92 7 3.53 g (s.g. 10.212).

ANONYMOUS   Mint: Rome. After 211 BC
Triens. Obv.: head of Minerva r.; above, ···· . Rev.: prow r.; above, ROMA ; below, ···· . Crawford 56/4.
62. 912x17.34 3 6 g.

Sextans. Obv.: head of Mercury r.; above, ·· . Rev.: prow r.; above, ROMA ; below, ·· . Crawford 56/6.
63. 969x134.189 1.5 7.82 g.

GRAIN-EAR.   Mint: Sicily. 211–208 BC
Quinarius. Obv.: head of Roma r.; behind, V . Rev.: Dioscuri on horseback r.; in exergue, ROMA in linear frame. Crawford 68/2b.
64. 912x17.38 5 1.95 g.

GRAIN-EAR   Mint: Sicily. 211–210 BC
Denarius. Obv.: head of Roma r.; behind, X . Rev.: Dioscuri on horseback r.; below, grain-ear; in exergue, ROMA in linear frame. Crawford 72/3.
65. 969x134.2 9 3.68 g. Broken. Obv.: from same die as Crawford pl. XIV.13. From same dies as Bank Leu (1977) taf. II.34.

STAFF   Mint: Sicily. 209–208 BC
Denarius. Obv.: head of Roma r.; behind, X . Rev.: Dioscuri on horseback r.; below, staff; in exergue, ROMA in linear frame. Crawford 78/1.
66. 912x17.37 3 4.20 g.

WHEEL   Mint: Sicily (?). 209–208 BC
Denarius serratus. Obv.: head of Roma r.; behind, X . Rev.: Dioscuri on horseback r.; below, wheel; in exergue, ROMA . Crawford 79/1.
67. 950.56.96 10 3.73 g.

DOLPHIN   Mint: Sicily (?). 209–208 BC
Denarius. Obv.: head of Roma r.; behind, X . Rev.: Dioscuri on horseback r.; below, dolphin; in exergue, ROMA . Crawford 80/1a.
68. 950.56.95 11 3.74 g.

H   Mint: S.E. Italy. 211–210 BC
Triens. Obv.: head of Minerva r.; above, ···· . Rev.: prow r.; above, ROMA ; before, H ; below, ···· . Crawford 85/4.
69. 912x17.32 1.5 12.07 g.

VB   Mint: uncertain. 211–208 BC
Victoriatus. Obv.: head of Jupiter r. Rev.: Victory r., crowning trophy; between, ᚹ ; in exergue, ROMA . Crawford 95/1a.
70. 912x17.35 11 2.85 g. Obv.: from same die as Crawford pl. XVII.14.

L   Mint: Luceria. 211–208 BC
Victoriatus. Obv.: head of Jupiter r. Rev.: Victory r., crowning trophy; between, L ; in exergue, ROMA. Crawford 97/1a.
71. 969x134.1 4.5 2.65 g. From same dies as Panvini Rosati (1966) tav. 8.70.

P   Mint: Luceria. 209–208 BC (perhaps later)
As. Obv.: head of Janus; above, ‒; below, P . Rev.: prow r.; above, I; before, P ; below, ROMA . Crawford 99/1a.
72. 969x134.176 1 29.73 g.

ROSTRUM TRIDENS   Mint: Rome. 206–195 BC
Denarius. Obv.: head of Roma r.; behind, X . Rev.: Dioscuri on horseback r.; below, *rostrum tridens*; in linear frame, ROMA. Crawford 114/1.
73. 969x134.5 6.5 3.37 g (s.g. 10.367).

TRIDENT   Mint: Rome. 206–195 BC
Denarius. Obv.: head of Roma r.; behind, X. Rev.: Dioscuri on horseback r.; below, trident; in linear frame, ROMA . Crawford 115/1.
74. 950.56.97 3 3.89 g.

PRAWN   Mint: Rome. 179–170 BC
Denarius. Obv.: head of Roma r.; behind, X . Rev.: Luna in fast biga r.; below, prawn; in linear frame, ROMA . Crawford 156/1.
75. 912x17.42 6 3.33 g (s.g. 10.429).

MAT   Mint: Rome. 179–170 BC
Victoriatus. Obv.: head of Jupiter r. Rev.: Victory r., crowning trophy; between, ᚼ ; in exergue, ROMA . Crawford 162/1a.
76. 950.56.98 12 2.46 g. Holed. Obv.: from a die by the same engraver as No. 59.

PAE   Mint: Rome. 169–158 BC
As. Obv.: head of Janus; above, I . Rev.: prow r.; above, Æ ; before, I ; below, ROMA . Crawford 176/1.
77. 924.3.222 11 24.54 g.

GRYPHON   Mint: Rome. 169–158 BC
Denarius. Obv.: head of Roma r.; behind, X . Rev.: Dioscuri on horseback r.; below, gryphon r.; in linear frame, ROMA . Crawford 182/1.
78. 912x17.44 1.5 3.92 g. Obv.: from same die as Crawford pl. XXIX.10.

PVR   Mint: Rome. 169–158 BC
Denarius. Obv.: head of Roma r.; behind, X . Rev.: Luna in fast biga r.; above, murex shell; below, PVR ; in linear frame, ROMA. Crawford 187/1.
79. 921.62.55 7 3.36 g (s.g. 10.445). Obv.: from same die as Bank Leu (1977) taf. IV.87. From same dies as Belloni (1960) tav. 21.484.

ANCHOR   Mint: Rome. 169–158 BC   For a placement of these with the denarii with anchor, Crawford 165, of 179–170 BC, see Hersh (1977) 29.
As. Obv.: head of Janus; above, I . Rev.: prow r.; above, I ; before, anchor; below, ROMA . Crawford 194/1.
80. 969x134.177 11 36 g.
81. 923.45.71 9 19.53 g. Obv.: very worn.
Semis. Obv.: head of Saturn r.; behind, S . Rev.: prow r.;

above, S ; before, anchor; below, ROMA . Crawford 194/2.
  82. 923.45.70 1.5 8.31 g.

ANONYMOUS   Mint: Rome. 157–156 BC
  Denarius. Obv.: head of Roma r.; behind, X . Rev.: Victory
  in fast biga r.; in exergue, ROMA . Crawford 197/1a.
  83. 950.56.99 8 3.72 g.
  84. 969x134.138 9 3.56 g (s.g. 10.407).

SAR   Mint: Rome. 155 BC
  Denarius. Obv.: head of Roma r.; behind, X . Rev.: Victory
  in fast biga r.; below, SAR ; in exergue, ROMA . Crawford
  199/1a.
  85. 950.56.100 4.5 3.76 g.

  Semis. Obv.: head of Saturn r.; behind, S . Rev.: prow r.;
  above, SAR ; before, S ; below, ROMA . Crawford 199/3.
  86. 924.3.223 7 11.08 g. Rev.: moneyer's name is
    very faint.

NAT   Mint: Rome. 155 BC
  Denarius. Obv.: head of Roma r.; behind, X . Rev.: Victory
  in fast biga r.; below, NAT ; in exergue, ROMA . Crawford
  200/1.
  87. 987.257.38 9 3.35 g (s.g. 9.66).
  88. 969x134.96 6 3.31 g (s.g. 10.297).
  89. 950.164.11 5 2.84 g (s.g. 10.248). Rev.: NAT.

C.SCR   Mint: Rome. 154 BC
  Denarius. Obv.: head of Roma r.; behind, X . Rev.: Dioscuri
  on horseback r.; below, C·SCR ; in exergue, ROMA .
  Crawford 201/1.
  90. 950.56.103 10.5 3.33 g (s.g. 10.262). Obv.: single-
    drop earring as *BMCRR* I 98.730.
  91. 969x134.149 5 3.19 g (s.g. 9.853).

C.TAL   Mint: Rome. 154 BC
  Denarius. Obv.: head of Roma r.; behind, X . Rev.: Victory
  in fast biga r.; below, C·TAL ; in exergue, ROMA . Crawford
  202/1a.
  92. 969x134.89 6 3.82 g. Obv.: from same die as
    BMCRR III pl. XXIII.4 and Busso Peus (1969) taf.
    I.8.

L.SAVF   Mint: Rome. 152 BC
  Denarius. Obv.: head of Roma r.; behind, X . Rev.: Victory
  in fast biga r.; below, L·SAVF; in exergue, ROMA . Crawford
  204/1.
  93. 921.62.41 2 3.35 g (s.g. 10.424). Punchmarks on
    obv. and rev.

SAFRA   Mint: Rome. 150 BC
  Denarius. Obv.: head of Roma r.; behind, X . Rev.: Victory
  in fast biga r.; below, SAFRA ; in exergue, ROMA .
  Crawford 206/1.
  94. 969x134.6 3 3.39 g (s.g. 10.447).

FLAVS   Mint: Rome. 150 BC
  Denarius. Obv.: head of Roma r.; behind, X . Rev.: Luna in
  fast biga r.; below, FLAVS ; in exergue, ROMA . Crawford
  207/1.
  95. 921.62.12 2.5 3.89 g. From same obv. and rev.
    dies as Crawford pl. XXXIII.9 and same obv. die as
    Owl Ltd. and McKenna (1980) pl. 2.20.
  96. 921.62.13 8 3.33 g (s.g. 10.418).

NATA   Mint: Rome. 149 BC
  Denarius. Obv.: head of Roma r.; behind, X . Rev.: Victory
  in fast biga r.; below, NATA ; in exergue, ROMA . Crawford
  208/1.
  97. 969x134.43 6.5 3.80 g.

L.ITI   Mint: Rome. 149 BC
  Denarius. Obv.: head of Roma r.; behind, X . Rev.: Dioscuri
  on horseback r.; below, L·ITI ; in exergue, ROMA . Crawford
  209/1.
  98. 950.56.105 11 3.46 g (s.g. 10.376). Rev: from
    same die as Niggeler (1966) taf. 17.799.

C.IVNI. C.F   Mint: Rome. 149 BC
  Denarius. Obv.: head of Roma r.; behind, X . Rev.: Dioscuri
  on horseback r.; below, C·IVNI·C·F ; in exergue, ROMA .
  Crawford 210/1.
  99. 950.56.102 5.5 4.28 g.
  100. 950.56.117 4 3.61 g (s.g. 10.485).

MAST AND SAIL   Mint: Rome. c. 155–149 BC (but see
  Crawford 752 where the female head on the prow-stem perhaps indicates this issue belongs with those of P.SVLA,
  Crawford 205).
  Semis. Obv.: head of Saturn r.; behind, S . Rev.: prow r.,
  with prow-stem decorated with female head; above, mast and
  sail; before, S ; below, ROMA. Crawford 213/2.
  101. 912x17.49 10 10.67 g.

M.ATILI SARAN   Mint: Rome. 148 BC
  Denarius. Obv.: head of Roma r.; behind, SARAN upwards;
  before, X. Rev.: Dioscuri on horseback r.; below, M·ATIL ;
  ROMA in linear frame. Crawford 214/1c.
  102. 950.56.101 1 4.08 g. Rev.: from same die as
    Belloni (1960) tav. 20.451 and Arslan (1983) 46.225.
    Ex O'Hagan Collection, Sotheby (1908) lot 977.

Q.MARC LIBO   Mint: Rome. 148 BC
  Denarius. Obv.: head of Roma r.; behind, LIBO downwards;
  before, X . Rev.: Dioscuri on horseback r.; below, Q·MRC;
  ROMA in exergue or in linear frame. Crawford 215/1.
  103. 969x134.80 4 3.71 g. Rev.: ROMA in exergue.
  104. 950.56.104 5 3.53 g. Rev.: ROMA in linear
    frame.

C.TER LVC   Mint: Rome. 147 BC
  Denarius. Obv.: head of Roma r.; behind, X and Victory r.,
  with wreath. Rev.: Dioscuri on horseback r.; below, C·TER·
  LVC ; in exergue, ROMA . Crawford 217/1.
  105. 950.56.107 1 3.77 g.

L.CVP   Mint: Rome. 147 BC
Denarius. Obv.: head of Roma r.; behind, cornucopiae; before, X . Rev.: Dioscuri on horseback r.; below, L·CVP ; in exergue, ROMA . Crawford 218/1.
  106. 950.56.106 10 3.52 g (s.g. 10.349).

C.ANTESTI   Mint: Rome. 146 BC
Denarius. Obv.: head of Roma r.; behind, puppy walking upwards; before, X . Rev.: Dioscuri on horseback r.; below, C·ÆST; in exergue, ROMA. Crawford 219/1a.
  107. 969x134.7 6 3.59 g (s.g. 10.441).

M.IVNI   Mint: Rome. 145 BC
Denarius. Obv.: head of Roma r.; behind, ass's head l.; before, X. Rev.: Dioscuri on horseback r.; below, M·IVN ; in exergue, ROMA . Crawford 220/1.
  108. 969x134.87 1 3.94 g.

L.IVLI   Mint: Rome. 141 BC
Denarius. Obv.: head of Roma r.; behind, XVI downwards. Rev.: Dioscuri on horseback r.; below, L·IVI ; in exergue, ROMA . Crawford 224/1.
  109. 912x17.39 2 3.72 g (s.g. 10.471).
    Publ.: Curry (1973) 333–34 as Sydenham 443 but No. 109 is not plated.

C.TITINI   Mint: Rome. 141 BC
Denarius. Obv.: head of Roma r.; behind, XVI downwards. Rev.: Victory in fast biga r.; below, C·TITINI ; in exergue, ROMA . Crawford 226/1b.
  110. 912x17.41 9.5 3.72 g. Obv.: necklace of pendants is blurred. From same dies as Bank Leu (1977) taf. V.121.

C.VAL C.F FLAC   Mint: Rome. 140 BC
Denarius. Obv.: head of Roma r.; behind, X . Rev.: Victory in fast biga r.; above, FLAC; below, C·VA·C·F; in exergue, ROMA . Crawford 228/2.
  111. 950.56.110 1 3.77 g. From same dies as Münzen und Medaillen (1982) 36.258.
  112. 950.56.275 3 3.12 g. Plated.
    Publ.: Curry (1973) 333–34 as Sydenham 440.

A.SPVRI   Mint: Rome. 139 BC
Denarius. Obv.: head of Roma r.; behind, X . Rev.: Luna in fast biga r.; below, A·SP VRI ; in exergue, ROMA . Crawford 230/1.
  113. 969x134.114 8 3.78 g.
  114. 969x134.152 5 3.61 g.

C.RENI   Mint: Rome. 138 BC
Denarius. Obv.: head of Roma r.; behind, X . Rev.: Juno in biga of goats r.; below, C·RENI ; in exergue, ROMA . Crawford 231/1.
  115. 969x134.145 5 3.70 g.
  116. 912x17.43 5 2.55 g. Plated.

CN.GELI   Mint: Rome. 138 BC
Denarius. Obv.: head of Roma r.; behind, X . Rev.: warrior and captive in quadriga r.; below, CN·GEL ; in exergue, ROMA . Crawford 232/1.

117. 908.55.16   6 3.83 g. Obv.: from same die as Schulman (1981) 44.170. Ex O'Hagan Collection, Sotheby (1908) lot 981.
118. 908.55.15   2 3.75 g. From same dies as Empire Coins (1987) lot 286. Ex O'Hagan Collection, Sotheby (1908) lot 981.

P.PAETVS   Mint: Rome. 138 BC
Denarius. Obv.: head of Roma r.; behind, X . Rev.: Dioscuri on horseback r.; below, P·P AETVS ; in exergue, ROMA . Crawford 233/1.
  119. 950.56.113 5 3.90 g.

TI.VETVR   Mint: Rome. 137 BC
Denarius. Obv.: bust of Mars r.; behind, X and TI·VE downwards. Rev.: oath-taking scene with two warriors and a youth holding a pig; above, ROMA . Crawford 234/1.
  120. 950.56.135 1 3.39 g (s.g. 10.126).

SEX.POM   Mint: Rome. 137 BC
Denarius. Obv.: head of Roma r.; behind, jug; before, X . Rev.: Faustulus to l. of she-wolf suckling twins in front of the *ficus Ruminalis* with three perching birds; at l., FOSTLVS downwards; at r., SEX·PO upwards; in exergue, ROMA . Crawford 235/1c.
  121. 950.56.115 6 3.73 g.

M.BAEBI Q.F TAMPIL   Mint: Rome. 137 BC
Denarius. Obv.: head of Roma l., wearing necklace of beads or pendants; behind, TAMP IL upwards; before, X . Rev.: Apollo in quadriga r.; below, ROMA ; in exergue, M·BAEB· Q·F . Crawford 236.
  122. 969x134.11 2 3.83 g. Crawford 236/1c. Obv.: necklace of beads.
  123. 969x134.12 11 3.80 g. Crawford 236/1d. Obv.: necklace of beads. Rev.: no arrow.

CN.LVCR TRIO   Mint: Rome. 136 BC
Denarius. Obv.: head of Roma r.; behind, TRIO downwards; before, X . Rev.: Dioscuri on horseback r.; below, CN·LVCR; in exergue, ROMA . Crawford 237/1a.
  124. 950.56.258 7 4.00 g. Obv.: earring as *BMCRR* III pl. XXVI.8.
  125. 950.56.112 10.5 3.93 g. Obv.: earring as No. 124.
  126. 969x134.95 5 3.86 g. Obv.: earring worn but likely as No. 124.
  127. 969x134.94 5 3.84 g. Obv.: earring as *BMCRR* III pl. XXVI.7; from same die as Herbert (1987) pl. 9.179.

C.SERVEILI M.F   Mint: Rome. 136 BC (for the placing of this issue after Crawford 240–42, see Hersh [1977] 27).
Denarius. Obv.: head of Roma r.; behind, wreath and ✳ ; below, ROMA . Rev.: Dioscuri riding apart, with spears reversed; in exergue, C·SERVEILI·M·F . Crawford 239/1.
  128. 950.56.270 1 3.77 g.
  129. 969x134.107 5 3.77 g.
  130. 950.56.134 3 2.71 g. Plated. Rev.: punchmark.
    Publ.: Curry (1973) 333–34 as Sydenham 525.

TI.MINVCI C.F AVGVRINI   Mint: Rome.   134 BC
Denarius. Obv.: head of Roma r.; behind, ✳ . Rev.: spiral
column surmounted by statue and flanked by two togate figures; above, ROMA ; on l., TI·MINVCI·C·F upwards; on r.,
AVGVRINI downwards. Crawford 243/1.
> **131.** 950.56.119 12 3.79 g.
> **132.** 969x134.82   6 3.52 g (s.g. 10.417). Obv.: from
> same die as Malloy (1977) lot 391.

M.MARCI MN.F   Mint: Rome.   134 BC
Denarius. Obv.: head of Roma r.; behind, modius; before, ✳ .
Rev.: Victory in biga r.; below, M·MR·C ROMA, divided by two
ears of grain. Crawford 245/1; for a revised sequence with
Crawford 245, 261, 266–67, 260, 268, 252–54, 258–59,
263–65, and 269, see Hersh (1977) 26–27.
> **133.** 969x134.104 11 3.65 g.
> **134.** 969x134.102   8 3.48 g (s.g. 9.994).
> **135.** 987.257.39   1 2.90 g (s.g. 10.242).

P.CALP   Mint: Rome.   133 BC
Denarius. Obv.: head of Roma r.; behind, ✳ . Rev.: goddess
in biga r., with Victory flying above to crown her; star on
flank of nearest horse; below, P·CALP ; in exergue, ROMA.
Crawford 247/1.
> **136.** 912x17.45 4.5 3.72 g. Bent. Rev.: probably from
> same die as Herbert (1987) pl. 10.192.

L.MINVCIV   Mint: Rome.   133 BC
Denarius. Obv.: head of Roma r.; behind, ✳ . Rev.: Jupiter
in quadriga r.; below, ROMA ; in exergue, L·MINVCI .
Crawford 248/1.
> **137.** 969x134.32 2 3.83 g. Obv.: from the same die as
> Gorini (1973) 36.140.

P.MAE ANT M.F.   Mint: Rome.   132 BC
Denarius. Obv.: head of Roma r.; behind, ✳ . Rev.: Victory
in quadriga r.; below, P·ME·AT ; in exergue, ROMA .
Crawford 249/1.
> **138.** 969x134.98 5.5 3.78 g.

M.FABRINI   Mint: Rome.   132 BC
Semis. Obv.: head of Saturn r.; behind, S . Rev.: prow r.;
above, M·FABR ; before, S ; below, ROMA . Crawford
251/1.
> **139.** 987.257.37 11 11.88 g.

L.POST ALB   Mint: Rome.   131 BC
Denarius. Obv.: head of Roma r.; behind, *apex*; before, ✳ .
Rev.: Mars in quadriga r.; below, L·P OST A·B ; in exergue,
ROMA . Crawford 252/1); for a different placement of this
issue, see Nos. 133–35.
> **140.** 908.55.51 7 3.80 g. From the same dies as *BMCRR*
> III pl. XXIX.13. Ex O'Hagan Collection, Sotheby
> (1908) lot 985.

L.OPEIMI   Mint: Rome.   131 BC (Mattingly [1982] 44, c. 128 BC)
Denarius. Obv.: head of Roma r.; behind, wreath; before, ✳ .
Rev.: Victory in quadriga r.; below, L·OP EIMI ; in exergue,
ROMA . Crawford 253/1; for a different placement of this
issue, see Nos. 133–35.
> **141.** 921.62.26 10 3.83 g.

M.VARGV   Mint: Rome.   130 BC
Denarius. Obv.: head of Roma r.; behind, M·VARG down-
wards; before, ✳ . Rev.: Jupiter in quadriga r.; in exergue,
ROMA . Crawford 257/1.
> **142.** 969x134.117 6.5 3.80 g.

SEX.IVLI CAISAR   Mint: Rome.   129 BC (Mattingly [1982]
44, c. 127 BC)
Denarius. Obv.: head of Roma r.; behind, anchor; before, ✳ .
Rev.: Cupid crowning Venus in biga r.; above, ROMA ;
below, SEX·IVI ; in exergue, CAISAR . Crawford 258/1; for
a different placement of this issue, see Nos. 133–35.
> **143.** 950.56.130 11 3.68 g (s.g. 10.462). Rev.: deep
> scratch where a whip may have been held by Venus.

Q.PILIPVS   Mint: Rome.   129 BC
Denarius. Obv.: head of Roma r.; behind, ✳ . Rev.: horseman galloping r.; behind, helmet with goat's horns; below,
Q·P ILIP VS; in exergue, ROMA . Crawford 259/1; for a different placement of this issue, see Nos. 133–35.
> **144.** 950.56.133 1.5 3.58 g (s.g. 10.385). Obv.: no star
> on flap of helmet.

T.CLOVLI   Mint: Rome.   128 BC
Denarius. Obv.: head of Roma r.; behind, wreath; below,
ROMA . Rev.: Victory in biga r.; below, ear of grain; in
exergue, T·CLOVLI. Crawford 260/1; for a different placement of this issue, see Nos. 133–35.
> **145.** 921.62.2 2 3.82 g.

CN.DOMIT   Mint: Rome.   128 BC (Mattingly [1982] 44, c.
131 BC)
Denarius. Obv.: head of Roma r.; behind, ear of grain;
before, ✳ . Rev.: Victory in biga r.; above, ROMA ; below,
man fighting lion; in exergue, CN·DOM . Crawford 261/1;
for a different placement of this issue, see Nos. 133–35.
> **146.** 950.56.116 2 3.81 g. Obv.: gash at lower r. Ex
> O'Hagan Collection, Sotheby (1908) lot 980.
> **147.** 987.257.40 9.5 3.75 g. From the same dies as
> Crawford pl. XXXVIII.2.

ANONYMOUS WITH ELEPHANT'S HEAD   Mint: Rome.
128 BC
Denarius. Obv.: head of Roma r.; behind, ✳ . Rev.: goddess
in biga r.; below, elephant's head with bell attached; below,
ROMA . Crawford 262/1; for the placement of this issue
between Crawford 257 and 245, see Hersh (1977) 27.
> **148.** 969x134.13 4.5 3.78 g.

M.METELLVS Q.F   Mint: Rome.   127 BC (Mattingly [1982]
44, c. 126 BC)
Denarius. Obv.: head of Roma r.; behind, ROMA upwards;
before, ✳ . Rev.: Macedonian shield decorated with elephant's head; around, M·METELLVS·Q·F . Crawford
263/1a; for a different placement of this issue, see Nos.
133–35.
> **149.** 950.56.132 6 3.75 g.
> **150.** 950.56.234 4 3.58 g (s.g. 10.131).

Semis. Obv.: laureate head of Saturn r., behind, S . Rev.:
prow r., inscribed M·METELLVS ; above, round Macedonian
shield; before, S ; below, ROMA . Crawford 263/3a.
151. 969x134.172 8 7.58 g.

C.SERVEILI Mint: Rome. 127 BC
Denarius. Obv.: head of Roma r.; behind, *lituus*; below,
ROMA ; before, ✳ . Rev.: battle between armed horsemen;
in exergue, C·SERVEIL . Crawford 264/1; for a different
placement of this issue, see Nos. 133–35.
152. 969x134.101 2 3.78 g.

Q.MAX Mint: Rome. 127 BC (Mattingly [1982] 44, c. 126 BC)
Denarius. Obv.: head of Roma r.; behind, ROMA downwards; before, ✳ , and Q·MX upwards. Rev.: cornucopiae
superimposed on thunderbolt, all within a wreath of barley,
wheat, and fruit. Crawford 265/1; for a different placement
of this issue, see Nos. 133–35.
   153. 908.55.12 8 3.65 g (s.g. 9.963). Ex O'Hagan
      Collection, Sotheby (1908) lot 980.

C.CASSI Mint: Rome. 126 BC (Mattingly [1982] 44, c. 131 BC)
Denarius. Obv.: head of Roma r.; behind, voting-urn and ✳ .
Rev.: Libertas in quadriga r.; below, C·CASSI ; in exergue,
ROMA. Crawford 266/1; for a different placement of this
issue, see Nos. 133–35.
   154. 950.56.122 4 3.68 g (s.g. 10.412). Ex O'Hagan
      Collection, Sotheby (1908) lot 978.

N.FABI PICTOR Mint: Rome. 126 BC
Denarius. Obv.: head of Roma r.; behind, ✳ . Rev.: Q.
Fabius Pictor seated l. on chair; beside, shield inscribed
Q·VIRIN ; on r., ·N·FABI upwards; on l., P ICTOR downwards; in exergue, ROMA . Crawford 268/1a; for a different
placement of this issue, see Nos. 133–35.
   155. 908.55.13 11 3.83 g. Ex O'Hagan Collection,
      Sotheby (1908) lot 980.

M.PORC LAECA Mint: Rome. 125 BC
Denarius. Obv.: head of Roma r.; behind, LAECA down-
wards; before, ✳ . Rev.: Libertas, crowned by flying
Victory, in quadriga r.; below, M·P·ORC ; in exergue,
ROMA. Crawford 270/1.
   156. 969x134.68 2 3.11 g. Plated.

Q.FABI LABEO Mint: Rome. 124 BC
Denarius. Obv.: head of Roma r.; behind, ROMA downwards; before, X and LABEO upwards. Rev.: Jupiter in
quadriga r.; below, *rostrum*; in exergue, Q·FABI . Crawford
273/1.
   157. 950.56.124   4.5 3.85 g. Obv.: from same die as
      Gorini (1973) 98.566.
   158. 969x134.52 10.5 3.84 g.
   159. 969x134.57 6 3.76 g.
   160. 969x134.56 9 3.71 g.
   161. 969x134.55 5 3.66 g. Holed.
   162. 950.56.243 4 3.66 g.
   163. 969x134.53 1 3.62 g.
   164. 969x134.54 7 3.61 g. Obv.: two(?) punchmarks.

C.CATO Mint: Rome. 123 BC (Mattingly [1982] 44, 123/120 BC)
Denarius. Obv.: head of Roma r.; behind, X . Rev.: Victory
in biga r.; below, C·CATO ; in exergue, ROMA . Crawford
274/1.
   165. 921.62.34 9 3.63 g.

M.FAN C.F Mint: Rome. 123 BC
Denarius. Obv.: head of Roma r.; behind, ROMA downwards; before, X . Rev.: Victory in quadriga r.; in exergue,
M·FA/·C·F . Crawford 275/1.
   166. 950.56.114 11 3.76 g.
   167. 969x134.73 11 3.65 g.
   168. 969x134.74 4 3.44 g (s.g. 10.306).
   169. 969x134.77 4.5 2.98 g (s.g. 10.292).

M.CARBO Mint: Rome. 122 BC
Denarius. Obv.: head of Roma r.; behind, branch; before, X .
Rev.: Jupiter in quadriga r.; below, M·CARBO ; in exergue,
ROMA . Crawford 276/1.
   170. 950.56.109 8 3.79 g.

C.PLVTI Mint: Rome. 121 BC
Denarius. Obv.: head of Roma r.; behind, X . Rev.: Dioscuri
r.; below, C·P·LVTI ; in exergue, ROMA . Crawford 278/1; for
a placement of Crawford 278 after 279, see Hersh (1977) 27.
   171. 969x134.48 4.5 3.84 g.
   172. 950.56.111 10 3.82 g. Rev.: from same die as
      Calicó (1983) 217.1.136.
   173. 969x134.47 1.5 3.76 g.

CARBO Mint: Rome. 121 BC (Mattingly [1982] 44, 123/120 BC)
Denarius. Obv.: head of Roma r.; behind, X . Rev.: Jupiter in
quadriga r.; below, CARB ; in exergue, ROMA . Crawford
279/1.
   174. 950.56.262 1.5 3.71 g.
   175. 950.56.108 8 3.70 g.

M.TVLLI Mint: Rome. 120 BC
Denarius. Obv.: head of Roma r.; behind, ROMA downwards. Rev.: Victory in quadriga r.; above, wreath; below, X ;
in exergue, M·TVLLI . Crawford 280/1.
   176. 969x134.116 1 3.79 g. Obv.: punchmark on cheek;
      from same die as Marek (1985) pl. XIV.47.
   177. 969x134.115 5 3.73 g. Probably from same dies as
      Herbert (1987) pl. 11.231.

M.FOVRI L.F PHILI Mint: Rome. 119 BC
Denarius. Obv.: head of Janus; around, M·FOVRI·L·F . Rev.:
Roma standing l., crowning trophy; above, star; behind,
ROMA upwards; in exergue, PHLI . Crawford 281/1.
   178. 950.56.252 10 3.74 g.
   179. 950.56.137 2 3.56 g (s.g. 10.309).

L.LIC, CN.DOM AND ASSOCIATES   Mint: Narbo (Rome, cf. Crawford [1984] 11.62). 118 BC (Mattingly [1982] 44, 118 or 114 BC?)
Denarius serratus. Obv.: head of Roma r.; around, L·CO⌣CO·M·F ; behind, X ; border of dots. Rev.: naked, bearded warrior in biga r.; in exergue, L·LIC·CN·DOM . Crawford 282/2.
   180. 950.56.238   1 3.83 g.
   181. 950.56.136   5 3.70 g.

Denarius serratus. Obv.: as above, but around, C·MALLE·C·F. Rev.: as above. Crawford 282/3.
   182. 950.56.138   5 3.86 g.

Denarius serratus. Obv.: as above, but around, L·P·ORCI·LICI ; behind, ✳ . Rev.: as above. Crawford 282/5.
   183. 908.55.36   4.5 2.60 g. Plated. Ex O'Hagan Collection, Sotheby (1908) lot 985.
   Publ.: Curry (1973) 333–34 as Sydenham 520.

Q.MAR, C.F, L.R   Mint: Rome. 118 or 117 BC
Denarius. Obv.: head of Roma r.; behind, ✳ . Rev.: Victory in quadriga r., holding reins in l. hand and wreath in r. hand; below, ROMA ; in exergue, Q·MR·C·F·L·R . Crawford 283/1a.
   184. 921.62.24   10 3.70 g.

M.CALID, Q.MET, CN.FOVL   Mint: Rome. 117 or 116 BC (Mattingly [1982] 44, c. 115 BC)
Denarius. Obv.: head of Roma r.; behind, ROMA downwards; before, ✳ . Rev.: Victory in biga r.; below, M·CALID ; in exergue, Q·ME·CNFL . Crawford 284/1a.
   185. 969x134.17   5 3.94 g.
   186. 969x134.18   5 3.72 g. Obv.: several punchmarks.

Denarius. Obv.: as above. Rev.: as above, but CNFOVL below and M·CA·Q·ME in exergue. Crawford 284/1b.
   187. 950.56.120   10 3.63 g (s.g. 10.467).

CN.DOMI, Q.CVRTI, M.SILA   Mint: Rome. 116 or 115 BC
Denarius. Obv.: head of Roma r.; before, ROMA upwards; behind, X. Rev.: Jupiter in quadriga r.; in exergue, CN·DOMI . Crawford 285/1.
   188. 950.56.118   8.5 3.77 g.
   189. 950.56.240   10.5 3.24 g (s.g. 10.358).

Denarius. Obv.: head of Roma r., usually with curl on left shoulder; before, Q·CVRT upwards; behind, X . Rev.: Jupiter in quadriga r.; above, *lituus*; below, M·SIA ; in exergue, ROMA . Crawford 285/2.
   190. 950.56.121   9 3.76 g. Obv.: no curl.
   191. 969x134.72   3 3.51 g (s.g. 10.377). Obv.: curl.

M.SERGI SILVS Q   Mint: Rome. 116 or 115 BC
Denarius. Obv.: head of Roma r.; before, EX·S·C ; behind, ROMA downwards and ✳ . Rev.: horseman l.; before, Q ; below, M·SERGI ; in exergue, SILVS . Crawford 286/1.
   192. 950.56.129   7 3.85 g.
   193. 950.56.269   7 3.73 g.

   194. 969x134.151   6 3.70 g.
   195. 969x134.150   7 3.50 g (s.g. 10.357).
   196. 950.56.128   12 3.81 g. Brockage.

ANONYMOUS   Mint: Rome. 115 or 114 BC
Denarius. Obv.: head of Roma r.; below, ROMA ; behind, X . Rev.: Roma seated r. with wolf suckling twins at r. and flying bird at l. and r. Crawford 287/1.
   197. 969x134.3   10 3.86 g. Rev.: die flaw in field above r. bird.
   198. 969x134.4   4.5 3.17 g. Plated.

M.CIPI M.F.   Mint: Rome. 115 or 114 BC
Denarius. Obv.: head of Roma r.; before, M·CIPI·M·F upwards; behind, X . Rev.: Victory in biga r.; below, rudder; in exergue, ROMA . Crawford 289/1.
   199. 908.55.10   2 3.87 g. Ex O'Hagan Collection, Sotheby (1908) lot 978.
   200. 908.55.9   11 3.84 g. Ex O'Hagan Collection, Sotheby (1908) lot 978.

C.FONT   Mint: Rome. 114 or 113 BC (Mattingly [1982] 44, c. 112 BC)
Denarius. Obv.: laureate janiform head of Dioscuri; on l. and below, control mark; on r., ✳ . Rev.: ship l.; above, C·FONT ; below, ROMA . Crawford 290/1.
   201. 950.56.140   2 3.75 g. Obv.: on l., C ; below neck, ... ; cf. *BMCRR* II 292:602.
   202. 950.56.246   7 3.50 g (s.g. 10.34). Obv.: illegible control marks.

P.NERVA   Mint: Rome. 113 or 112 BC
Denarius. Obv.: bust of Roma l.; above, crescent; behind, ROMA upwards; before, ✳ . Rev.: voting scene; above, P·NERVA ; at top, bar and tablet bearing letter P . Crawford 292/1.
   203. 950.56.127   1 3.73 g. Obv.: punchmark across ear.
   204. 950.56.126   7 2.87 g. Plated; hole at centre. Publ.: Curry (1973) 333–34 as Sydenham 548.

L.PHILIPPVS   Mint: Rome. 113 or 112 BC (Mattingly [1982] 44, c. 110 BC)
Denarius. Obv.: male head r. (Philip V of Macedon); behind, AA downwards; before, Φ . Rev.: equestrian statue r.; below, on tablet, L·P·HILIPPVS ; below, ✳ . Crawford 293/1.
   205. 969x134.105   4.5 3.85 g.
   206. 969x134.106   2 3.73 g.

L.TORQVA Q   Mint: Rome. 113 or 112 BC
Denarius. Obv.: head of Roma r.; behind, ROM downwards; before, X ; torque as border. Rev.: horseman charging l.; below, L·TORQVA ; above, Q ; in exergue, EX·S·C . Crawford 295/1.
   207. 921.62.23   9 3.18 g (s.g. 10.271). Rev.: die flaw over exergual line.

CN.BLASIO CN.F   Mint: Rome. 112 or 111 BC
Denarius. Obv.: head of Mars r.; above, ✳ ; before, CN·BLASIO·CN·F ; behind, bucranium. Rev.: Jupiter stand-

ing between Juno and Minerva who is crowning him; in field, Θ ; below, ROMA . Crawford 296/1c.
208. 969x134.29 5 3.78 g.

Denarius. Obv.: as above but prow-stem behind. Rev.: as above but ᴨ in field. Crawford 296/1d.
209. 950.56.146 6 3.87 g.

TI.Q Mint: Rome. 112 or 111 BC
Denarius. Obv.: bust of Hercules. Rev.: *desultor* l.; behind, control mark; below, rat l. between TI Q ; in exergue, incuse on tablet, D·S·S . Crawford 297/1a.
    210. 950.56.143 12 3.54 g (s.g. 10.126). Obv.: all that is present of the laurel wreath is a ribbon lying over the neck. Rev.: the control mark is illegible and the Q is not present.

Denarius. Obv.: as above. Rev.: as above, but rat r. Crawford 297/1b.
    211. 950.56.267 3.5 3.83 g. Rev.: control mark, Ḷ as *BMCRR* II 289.575. From same dies as Münzen und Medaillen (1970) pl. 9.85.
    212. 969x134.144 2.5 3.35 g (s.g. 10.447). Obv.: punchmarks in front of chin. Rev.: control mark, Y· ; punchmark at r.

L. CAESI Mint: Rome. 112 or 111 BC
Denarius. Obv.: bust of Apollo; on r., Å . Rev.: Lares Praestites seated with dog between and above, bust of Vulcan; on l., A ; on r., Ʀ ; in exergue, L·CÆSI . Crawford 298/1.
    213. 969x134.16 1 3.91 g. From same dies as Bank Leu (1977) taf. IX.211.

AP.CL, T.MAL or T.MANL, Q.VR Mint: Rome. 111 or 110 BC
Denarius. Obv.: head of Roma r.; behind, quadrangular device. Rev.: Victory in triga r.; in exergue, AP·CL·T·M·Q·VR . Crawford 299/1a.
    214. 950.56.237 2 3.73 g. Obv.: punchmark on temple.
    215. 950.56.139 3 3.41 g (s.g. 10.565).

C.PVLCHER Mint: Rome. 110 or 109 BC (Mattingly [1982] 44, c. 106 BC)
Denarius. Obv.: head of Roma r. Rev.: Victory in biga r.; in exergue, C·P·VLCHER . Crawford 300/1.
    216. 921.62.57 7.5 3.77 g.

P.LAECA Mint: Rome. 110 or 109 BC
Denarius. Obv.: head of Roma r.; above, ROMA ; behind, P·LÆCA downwards; before, X . Rev.: figure in military dress with togate figure on l. and attendant with rods on r.; in exergue, P·ROVOCO . Crawford 301/1.
    217. 950.56.156 7.5 3.90 g. Obv.: die flaw on eye.
    218. 950.56.264 9.5 3.85 g.

L.FLAMINI CILO Mint: Rome. 109 or 108 BC
Denarius. Obv.: head of Roma r.; behind, ROMA downwards; before, X . Rev.: Victory in biga r.; below, L·FLAMINI ; in exergue, CILO . Crawford 302/1.

219. 969x134.61 6 3.86 g.
220. 969x134.62 2 3.80 g.

MN.AQVIL Mint: Rome. 109 or 108 BC (Mattingly [1982] 44, c. 108/7 BC)
Denarius. Obv.: head of Sol r.; before, X . Rev.: Luna in biga r., with three stars above; below, one star and M·AQVIL ; in exergue, ROMA . Crawford 303/1.
    221. 950.56.164 11 3.64 g. Ex O'Hagan Collection, Sotheby (1908) lot 977.

L.MEMMI Mint: Rome. 109 or 108 BC
Denarius. Obv.: young male head r. (?Apollo); before, ✱ . Rev.: Dioscuri; in exergue, L·MEMMI . Crawford 304/1.
    222. 950.56.160 7 3.63 g.

Q.LVTATI CERCO Q Mint: Rome. 109 or 108 BC
Denarius. Obv.: head of Roma r.; above, ROMA ; before, CERCO upwards; behind, ✱ . Rev.: ship r.; above, Q·LVATI .
Crawford 305/1.   Q
    223. 921.62.21 2 3.60 g.

L.VALERI FLACCI Mint: Rome. 108 or 107 BC (Mattingly [1982] 44, c. 108/7 BC)
Denarius. Obv.: bust of Victory r., draped; before, ✱ . Rev.: Mars walking l.; before, *apex*; behind, ear of grain; on l., L·VALERI FLACCI downwards. Crawford 306/1.
    224. 950.56.276 3 3.80 g.
    225. 969x134.154 12.5 3.79 g.
    226. 950.56.150 3 3.63 g (s.g. 10.516).

MN.FONTEI Mint: Rome. 108 or 107 BC
Denarius. Obv.: jugate heads of Dioscuri r.; below their chins, ✱ . Rev.: ship r.; above, M·FONEI ; below, control mark and two or three dots (see Hersh [1977] 29.307). Crawford 307/1c.
    227. 950.56.141 3 3.84 g. Rev.: control mark, ·( ) . Ex O'Hagan Collection, Sotheby (1908) lot 980.
    228. 950.56.247 12 3.80 g. Brockage. Ex O'Hagan Collection, Sotheby (1908) lot 980.

M.HERENNI Mint: Rome. 108 or 107 BC (Mattingly [1982] 45, c. 105 BC)
Denarius. Obv.: head of Pietas r.; behind, P·IETAS downwards; before, control mark. Rev.: one of the Catanaean brothers running r., with his father on his shoulders (Aeneas rescuing his father from Troy, see Evans [1987] 116.n.45); on l., M·HERENNI downwards. Crawford 308/1a.
    229. 950.56.147 11 3.66 g (s.g. 10.253). Obv.: control mark, Ó ; line border. Ex O'Hagan Collection, Sotheby (1908) lot 981.

A.MANLI Q.F SER Mint: Rome. 118–107 BC (Mattingly [1982] 44, c. 118 BC)
Denarius. Obv.: head of Roma r.; behind, SER downwards; before, ROMA upwards. Rev.: Sol in quadriga; on either side, star; on r., crescent; on l., X ; below, waves and A·MNLI·Q·F . Crawford 309/1.
    230. 921.62.22 3 2.81 g. Plated.

L.SCIP ASIAG   Mint: Rome.   106 BC (Mattingly [1982] 45, 104/3 BC)
Denarius serratus. Obv.: head of Jupiter l.; before, control mark. Rev.: Jupiter in quadriga r.; in exergue, L·SCIP·ASIAG . Crawford 311/1b.
> **231.** 950.56.145   6 2.95 g. Plated. Obv.: control mark, R· . Publ.: Curry (1975) 284–85 as Sydenham 576c.

L.COT   Mint: Rome.   105 BC
Denarius serratus. Obv.: bust of Vulcan r.; before, control mark; behind, ✳ ; around, wreath. Rev.: eagle on thunderbolt r.; below, L·COT ; around, laurel wreath. Crawford 314/1b.
> **232.** 908.55.3   3 3.58 g (s.g. 10.276). Obv.: control mark, V̈ . Ex O'Hagan Collection, Sotheby (1908) lot 977.
> **233.** 950.56.144   5 3.45 g. Plated. Obv.: control mark, D . Rev.: probably taken from a denarius from the same die as Adolph Hess (1970) taf.XX.426. Ex O'Hagan Collection, Sotheby (1908) lot 977.

L.THORIVS BALBVS   Mint: Rome.   105 BC (Mattingly [1982] 45, c. 102 BC)
Denarius. Obv.: head of Juno Sospita r.; behind, I·S·M·R downwards. Rev.: bull charging r.; above, control mark; below, L·THORIVS ; in exergue, BALBVS . Crawford 316/1.
> **234.** 950.56.272   5 3.84 g. Rev.: control mark, A as *BMCRR* III pl. XXXI.22.
> **235.** 950.56.271   5 3.80 g. Rev.: as No. 234.
> **236.** 950.56.158   4.5 3.77 g. Obv.: graffito scratched between border and edge, IVNIIA . Rev.: control mark, R as *BMCRR* I 226.1634.
> **237.** 950.56.157   10 2.74 g. Plated. Rev.: as No. 234.

L.SATVRN   Mint: Rome.   104 BC (Mattingly [1977] 205 and [1982] 35 and 45, 101 BC but Crawford reaffirms his dating of 104 BC, see Carson, Berghaus and Lowick [1979] 173)
Denarius. Obv.: head of Roma r. Rev.: Saturn in quadriga r.; below, control mark and L·SATVRN . Crawford 317/3b.
> **238.** 950.56.233   7 3.73 g. Rev.: control mark, ➤ . Ex O'Hagan Collection, Sotheby (1908) lot 977.
> **239.** 950.56.161   10 3.77 g. Rev.: control mark, S . Ex O'Hagan Collection, Sotheby (1908) lot 977.

C.COIL CALD   Mint: Rome.   104 BC (Mattingly [1982] 45, 101 BC)
Denarius. Obv.: head of Roma l. Rev.: Victory in biga l.; above, control mark; below, C·COIL ; in exergue, CALD . Crawford 318/1a.
> **240.** 921.62.3   1 3.74 g. Rev.: control mark, ·T as *BMCRR* I 213.1459.

Denarius. Obv.: as above. Rev.: as above but below, CALD ; in exergue, control mark. Crawford 318/1b.
> **241.** 969x134.38   4.5 3.69 g (s.g. 10.347). Rev.: control mark, ·A . From same dies as *BMCRR* III pl. XXXI.13.

> **242.** 969x134.39   5.5 3.08 g. Plated. Rev.: control mark, ·B· .

Q.THERM M.F   Mint: Rome.   103 BC (Mattingly [1982] 35 and 45, 99 BC but the moneyer has to be linked with L. Caesar)
Denarius. Obv.: head of Mars l. Rev.: Roman fighting barbarian over fallen comrade; in exergue, Q·THERM·MF . Crawford 319/1.
> **243.** 950.56.153   12 3.63 g (s.g. 10.237).

L.IVLI L.F CAESAR   Mint: Rome.   103 BC (Mattingly [1982] 45, 99 BC but Crawford points out that since L. Caesar was consul in 90, he could hardly have been moneyer in the 90s, see Carson, Berghaus and Lowick [1979] 173)
Denarius. Obv.: head of Mars l.; behind, CAESAR upwards; above, control mark. Rev.: Venus in biga of Cupids l.; above, control mark; below, lyre; in exergue, L·IVLI·L·F . Crawford 320/1.
> **244.** 969x134.84   5 3.88 g. Obv. and rev.: control mark, B .
> **245.** 950.56.159   7 3.81 g. Obv. and rev.: control mark, L .
> **246.** 969x134.83   7 3.93 g. Obv. and Rev.: control mark, ⸲ .
> **247.** 950.56.253   6.5 3.07 g. Plated. Obv. and rev. control marks, Q/Ọ , noted by M. Crawford, see Crawford 563.270.

L.CASSI CAEICIAN   Mint of Rome.   102 BC
Denarius. Obv.: bust of Ceres l.; behind, CÆICIAN upwards; above, control mark. Rev.: yoke of oxen l.; above, control mark; in exergue, L·CASSI . Crawford 321/1.
> **248.** 950.56.167   6.5 3.86 g. Obv.: control mark, B . Rev.: control mark, V . Cf. *BMCRR* I 237.1727.

C.FABI C.F   Mint: Rome.   102 BC (Mattingly [1982] 45, 100 BC)
Denarius. Obv.: bust of Cybele r.; behind, control mark. Rev.: Victory in biga r.; below, bird; in exergue, C·FABI·C·F . Crawford 322/1a.
> **249.** 969x134.75   7 3.60 g (s.g. 10.454). Obv: control mark, I .
> **250.** 950.56.154   5.5 3.86 g. Obv.: control mark, Φ . From same dies as *BMCRR* III pl. XXXI.19.

Denarius. Obv.: as above, but behind, EX·A·P·V upwards; no control mark. Rev.: as above, but control mark l. of bird. Crawford 322/1b.
> **251.** 950.56.155   10.5 3.92 g. Rev.: control mark, A· as *BMCRR* I 223.1592.
> **252.** 950.56.245   12.5 3.64 g (s.g. 10.443). Rev.: control mark, T .
> **253.** 950.56.244   7 3.94 g. Rev.: control mark, V ; from same die as Auctiones (1977) 38.543.

M.LVCILI RVF   Mint: Rome. 101 BC
Denarius. Obv.: head of Roma r.; behind, Ρ V downwards.
Rev.: Victory in biga r.; below, M·LVCILI ; above, RVF .
Crawford 324/1.
>   **254.** 969x134.93 6 3.83 g.
>   **255.** 969x134.91 6.5 3.75 g.
>   **256.** 969x134.92 4.5 3.73 g.

L.SENTI C.F   Mint: Rome. 101 BC
Denarius. Obv.: head of Roma r.; behind, ARGΡ VB downwards. Rev.: Jupiter in quadriga r.; below, control mark;
below, L·SENTI·C·F . Crawford 325/1b.
>   **257.** 921.62.46 5.5 3.11 g. Plated. Rev.: control mark
>   broken away.
>   Publ.: Curry (1973) 333–34 as Sydenham 600.

C.FVNDAN Q   Mint: Rome. 101 BC (Mattingly [1982] 41, 90s
BC)
Denarius. Obv.: head of Roma r.; behind, control mark. Rev.:
triumphator in quadriga r., with rider on near horse; above, Q
; in exergue, C·FVNDAN . Crawford 326/1.
>   **258.** 950.56.168 7 3.90 g. Obv.: control mark, ·R as
>   *BMCRR* I 232.1693.

Quinarius. Obv.: head of Jupiter r.; behind, control mark.
Rev.: Victory r. crowning trophy with kneeling captive at
base; on r., C·FVNDA upwards; in exergue, Q . Crawford
326/2.
>   **259.** 969x134.66   5   1.85 g (s.g. 9.902). Obv.: control
>   mark, A .
>   **260.** 969x134.65   5   1.78 g (s.g. 9.548). Obv.: control
>   mark, Ρ . From same dies as Gorini (1973) 48.223
>   where the control mark is referred to as C but more of
>   the mark is on the flan on No. 260.

M.SERVEILI C.F   Mint: Rome. 100 BC
Denarius. Obv.: head of Roma r.; behind, control mark. Rev.:
two soldiers fighting on foot, their horses in the background;
in exergue, M·SERVEILI·C·F ; below, control mark. Crawford
327/1.
>   **261.** 950.56.169 2 3.80 g. Obv.: control mark, Δ. Rev.:
>   control mark, X . Cf. *BMCRR* I 230.1671.

P.SERVILI M.F. RVLLI   Mint: Rome. 100 BC
Denarius. Obv.: bust of Minerva l.; behind, RV L L I upwards.
Rev.: Victory in biga r.; below, Ρ ; in exergue,   Ρ·SERVILI·
M·F . Crawford 328/1.
>   **262.** 921.62.47 6 3.80 g.

PISO, CAEPIO Q   Mint: Rome. 100 BC
Denarius. Obv.: head of Saturn r.; behind, *harpa*; around (,
Ρ ISO·CAEΡ IO·Q ; above, control mark. Rev.: two male figures seated on bench (*subsellium*); to l. and r., ear of grain; in
exergue, AD·FRV·EMV / EX·S·C . Crawford 330/1b.
>   **263.** 950.56.125 6 3.81 g. Obv.: control mark, hare, as
>   Crawford pl. XLII.22 but with punchmark over it.
>   From same dies as Münzen und Medaillen (1975) pl.
>   20.320.

P.SABIN Q   Mint: Rome. 99 BC (Mattingly [1982] 41, 90s BC)
Quinarius. Obv.: head of Jupiter r.; behind, control mark.
Rev.: Victory r., crowning trophy; between, Ρ·SABIN down-
wards; in exergue, Q ; on r., control mark. Crawford 331/1.
>   **264.** 950.56.162 12 1.69 g. Obv. and rev.: control marks,
>   Ṗ/Ρ (?).
>   **265.** 969x134.155 7 1.73 g. Obv. and rev.: illegible con-
>   trol mark.

C.EGNATVLEI C.F Q   Mint: Rome. 97 BC (Mattingly [1982]
41, 90s BC)
Quinarius. Obv.: head of Apollo r.; behind, C·EGATVLEI·C·F·Q
downwards. Rev.: Victory l., inscribing shield attached to trophy; between Victory and trophy, Q ; in exergue, ROMA .
Crawford 333.
>   **266.** 950.56.241 10.5 1.91 g.
>   **267.** 950.56.242 6 1.81 g.
>   **268.** 950.56.123 10.5 1.62 g.

C.MALL, A.ALBINVS S.F, L.METEL   Mint: Rome. ?96 BC
(Mattingly [1982] 41, 91 BC)
Denarius. Obv.: head of Apollo r.; before, A·ALB·S·F
upwards; behind, L·METEL downwards; below, star. Rev.:
Roma seated l., being crowned by Victory; on l., C·MA·L
downwards; in exergue, ROMA . Crawford 335/1b.
>   **269.** 969x134.14 7 3.68 g.
>   **270.** 969x134.15 10 3.51 g.

Denarius. Obv.: head of Mars r.; above, hammer; before, ✳ .
Rev.: warrior standing l., holding spear and placing r. foot on
cuirass; on l., trophy; on r., prow; above prow, C·MA·L
upwards. Crawford 335/3b.
>   **271.** 950.56.170 10 3.62 g.

Denarius. Obv.: bust of Diana r.; below, ROMA . Rev.: three
horsemen charging l. towards a fallen warrior; in exergue, A·
ALBINVS·S·F . Crawford 335/9.
>   **272.** 950.56.165 8 3.66 g.

Denarius. Obv.: head of Apollo r.; behind, star with eight rays;
below, ROMA ; before, X . Rev.: Dioscuri at fountain of
Juturna; in field, crescent; in exergue, A·ALBINVS·S·F .
Crawford 335/10a.
>   **273.** 950.56.166 11 3.77 g. Obv.: from the same die as
>   Herbert (1987) pl. 14.359, which is by the same
>   engraver as Carson (1971) 17-8.23, also with an
>   eight-rayed star.

D.SILANVS L.F   Mint: Rome. 91 BC (Mattingly [1977] 203,
90 BC)
Denarius. Obv.: head of Salus r.; below, SA·VS ; before, control mark. Rev.: Victory in biga r.; below, ROMA ; in exergue,
D·SILANVS·L·F . Crawford 337/2c.
>   **274.** 921.62.19 10 4.18 g. Obv.: control mark, Ɔ .

Denarius. Obv.: as above, but below, SALVS and before, Ρ .
Rev.: as above, but below, control mark instead of ROMA .
Crawford 337/2f.
>   **275.** 969x134.128   11   3.87 g. Rev.: control symbol,
>   grasshopper.

Denarius. Obv.: head of Roma r.; behind, control mark. Rev.: Victory in biga r.; above, control mark; in exergue, D·SILANVS·L·F ROMA . Crawford 337/3.

276. 950.56.255   6   3.88 g. Obv.: control mark, B ; die flaws on front of head and mouth. Rev.: control mark, V ; D·SILANVS·L ; Belloni (1960) 108.1009.

277. 987.257.41   11   4.12 g. Obv.: control mark, Ɔ . Rev.: control mark, VIII (?) or VIIII with last numeral off flan; D·SILANVS . The combination of D and VIIII occurs on *BMCRR* I 245.1780.

278. 950.56.171   1.5   3.73 g. Obv.: control mark, K . Rev.: control mark, XIII ; D·SILANVS (?).

279. 950.56.256   7   3.30 g. Plated. Obv.: control mark, L . Rev.: control mark, II ; D·SILANVS·L·F .

L.PISO L.F. L.N FRVGI   Mint: Rome. 90 BC
Denarius. Obv.: head of Apollo r.; control marks. Rev.: horseman galloping r.; below horse, L·P ISOFRVGI ; control marks. Crawford 340/1.

280. 969x134.10   5.5   3.95 g. Obv.: control marks, hammer and O . Rev.: control marks, flute as *BMCRR* I 251-2.n.1, symbol 69 and V .

281. 969x134.19   1.5   3.70 g (s.g. 9.932). Obv.: control marks, hammer and R , with partial letter in r. field. Rev.: E and horizontal staff as *BMCRR* I 251-2.n.1, symbol 73; from same die as Bank Leu (1977) taf. XIV.333 with dagger and three dots on obv. From same dies as Belloni (1960) tav. 35.1170.

282. 969x134.21   10.5   3.95 g. Obv.: control mark, R . Rev.: control mark, H .

283. 950.56.172   9   3.85 g. Obv.: control mark, trident. Rev.: control mark, XXXXII .

284. 969x134.20   1   3.82 g. Obv.: control mark, CXXIII . Rev.: control marks, C↲— and *R* . From same dies as Herbert (1987) pl. 15.378 and Bank Leu (1977) taf. XIV.316.

285. 969x134.22   1.5   2.99 g. Plated. Obv.: any control marks are illegible. Rev.: control mark, ↓XIII .

Q.TITI   Mint: Rome. 90 BC (Mattingly [1982] 42, 89 BC)
Denarius. Obv: bearded head r. Rev.: Pegasus r.; below, in linear frame, Q·TITI . Crawford 341/1.

286. 950.56.176   9   3.68 g.

287. 969x134.153   7   3.61 g.

Denarius. Obv.: head of Liber r. Rev.: as above. Crawford 341/2.

288. 921.62.50   4   3.94 g. From same dies as Lanz (1988) taf. 19.377.

289. 921.62.51   5   3.00 g (s.g. 9.836).

Quinarius. Obv.: bust of Victory r. Rev.: Pegasus r.; below, Q·TITI . Crawford 341/3.

290. 950.56.231   10   1.80 g.

C.VIBIVS C.F. PANSA   Mint: Rome. 90 BC (Mattingly [1982] 42, 89 BC)
Denarius. Obv.: head of Apollo r.; behind, ꟼ ANSA downwards; before, control mark. Rev.: Ceres walking r.; before, pig; behind, C·VIBIVS·C·F downwards. Crawford 342/3b.

291. 969x134.118   11   3.44 g (s.g. 10.213). Obv.: control symbol, wreath.

Denarius. Obv.: as above. Rev.: Minerva in quadriga r.; in exergue, C·VIBIVS·C·F . Crawford 342/5b.

292. 921.62.52   7   4.00 g. Obv.: control symbol, thunderbolt(?) as *BMCRR* I 292.2272.

293. 950.56.177   5.5   3.75 g. Obv.: control symbol, caduceus tied with fillet; from a die by Buttrey's engraver F, see Buttrey (1976) 90–93.

294. 921.62.53   11   3.60 g (s.g. 10.358). Obv.: control symbol, prow.

295. 950.56.277   5   3.88 g. Obv.: control mark off flan; from a die by engraver F, see No. 293.

M.CATO   Mint: Rome. 89 BC
Denarius. Obv.: draped female bust r.; behind, ROMA ; below, M·CAͲO . Rev.: Victory seated r.; below seat, ST ;in exergue, VICͲRIX . Crawford 343/1c.

296. 950.56.151   12   3.64 g.

Quinarius. Obv.: head of Liber r.; behind, M·CAͲO downwards; below, control mark. Rev.: as above, but without ST . Crawford 343/2b.

297. 950.56.265   4.5   2.02 g. Obv.: control mark, II .

298. 969x134.50   3   2.02 g. Obv.: control mark, III(?) as *BMCRR* II 304.673.

299. 950.56.152   2   1.95 g. Obv.: control symbol, thunderbolt as *BMCRR* II 305.n.1.

L.TITVRI L.F SABINVS   Mint: Rome. 89 BC (Mattingly [1982] 42, 88 BC)
Denarius. Obv.: head of King Tatius r.; before, Ā or palmbranch; behind, SABIN downwards. Rev.: rape of the Sabine women; in exergue, L·TITVRI . Crawford 344/1a-b.

300. 950.56.173   7   3.86 g. Obv.: Ā or palm branch off flan.

Denarius. Obv.: as above, but without Ā or palm branch. Rev.: Victory in biga r.; below, L·TITVRI ; in exergue, control mark. Crawford 344/3.

301. 950.56.274   5.5   3.71 g. Rev.: control mark, IꓭB . From same dies as Herbert (1987) pl. 16.419.

302. 950.56.273   7   3.36 g (s.g. 9.65). Rev.: control symbol, rudder(?) as *BMCRR* I 299.2337.

303. 921.62.56   1   3.25 g. Plated. Rev.: control mark off flan.

CN.LENTVL   Mint: Rome. 88 BC
Denarius. Obv.: bust of Mars seen from behind. Rev.: Victory in biga r.; in exergue, CN·LENTVL . Crawford 345/1.

304. 969x134.58   4   3.61 g (s.g. 9.991).

305. 950.56.180   5   3.51 g (s.g. 10.25).

306. 969x134.59   11   3.46 g (s.g. 9.734).

Quinarius. Obv.: head of Jupiter r. Rev.: Victory r., crowning trophy; in exergue, CN·LENT or CN·LENͲ . Crawford 345/2.

307. 969x134.45   2   1.92 g.

C.CENSORIN   Mint: Rome. 88 BC
Denarius. Obv.: jugate heads of Numa Pompilius, bearded, and Ancus Marcius, not bearded, r. Rev.: *desultor* r.; below, control numeral; in exergue, C·CENSO . Crawford 346/1b.
308. 950.56.174   8 3.60 g. Rev.: control numeral, II as *BMCRR* I 302.2381 and Crawford (1971) 145.rev. die 25.
Denarius. Obv.: head of Apollo r. Rev.: horse galloping r.; below, C·CENSORI ; above and in exergue, control marks. Crawford 346/2b.
309. 950.56.175   10 3.44 g (s.g. 9.731). Rev.: control symbols, palm branch with two wreaths, above, and trident in exergue, as Crawford table XXVII.
310. 969x134.81   2 3.20 g (s.g. 10.172). Rev.: control marks, two arrows, above, and XX(XI) (following Crawford table XXVII) in exergue; C·CENSOR .

L.RVBRI DOSSEN   Mint: Rome. 87 BC
Denarius. Obv.: head of Jupiter r.; below, DOSSEN . Rev.: triumphal quadriga r.; above, Victory with wreath; in exergue, L·RVBRI . Crawford 348/1.
311. 950.56.163   7 4.09 g.
312. 950.56.178   5 3.83 g.

Denarius. Obv.: head of Juno r.; behind, DOS downwards. Rev.: as above, but eagle on thunderbolt on side panel. Crawford 348/2.
313. 950.56.268   11 3.94 g.
314. 969x134.148   5.5 3.55 g (s.g. 10.117).

Denarius. Obv.: bust of Minerva r.; behind, DOS downwards. Rev.: as above, but above, Victory in biga. Crawford 348/3.
315. 969x134.90   5 3.14 g (s.g. 10.021).

Quinarius. Obv.: head of Neptune r.; behind, D O S   S E N downwards. Rev.: Victory standing r.; before, garlanded altar with snake coiled around top; behind, L·RVBRI downwards. Crawford 348/4.
316. 950.56.179   10 2.10 g. Ex O'Hagan Collection, Sotheby (1908) lot 986.

GAR, OGVL, VER   Mint: Rome. 86 BC
Denarius. Obv.: head of Apollo r.; below, thunderbolt. Rev.: Jupiter in quadriga r.; above, control mark; below, GAR ; in exergue, OGV·VER . Crawford 350A/1a.
317. 950.56.184   5 3.90 g. Rev.: control mark, H as Crawford Table XXVIII.

Denarius. Obv.: as above. Rev.: as above, but no control mark or legend. Crawford 350A/2.
318. 969x134.40   2 3.94 g.
319. 969x134.41   6 3.68 g.
320. 973.296.87   6 3.32 g (s.g. 9.555).

M.FAN, L.CRIT AED.PL   Mint: Rome. 86 BC (Mattingly [1982] 42, c. 85 BC)
Denarius. Obv.: bust of Ceres r.; behind, AED·PL downwards. Rev.: two male figures seated on bench (*subsellium*);

on l., P·A ; on right, ear of grain; in exergue, M·FAN·L·CRt . Crawford 351/1.
321. 908.55.11   10 4.00 g. Obv.: from a die by Buttrey's engraver G, see Buttrey (1976) 90–93. From the same dies as Sydenham pl. 21.717. Ex O'Hagan Collection, Sotheby (1908) lot 980.

L.IVLI BURSIO   Mint: Rome. 85 BC
Denarius. Obv.: male head r., with attributes of Apollo, Mercury, and Neptune; behind, control mark. Rev.: Victory in quadriga r.; in exergue, L·IVLI·BVRSIO . Crawford 352/1a.
322. 969x134.85   6.5 3.75 g. Obv.: only a portion of a control mark, possibly a cornucopiae (see de Ruyter [1996] fig. 1.145), is on the flan; from a die by Buttrey's engraver G, see Buttrey (1976) 90–93.

Denarius. Obv.: as above. Rev.: as above, but control mark in field. Crawford 352/1c.
323. 969x134.86   7 3.81 g. Obv.: control symbol, arrow, see de Ruyter (1996) fig. 1.16; from same die as de Ruyter (1966) pl. 22.1 (obv. die 16). Rev.: control mark, DI . The obv. dies used for Nos. 323–25 are by Buttrey's engraver G, see Buttrey (1976) 90–93. From same dies as Lanz (1989) taf. 22.472; de Ruyter (1996) 131, die linkage 103.
324. 950.56.254   10 3.70 g. Obv.: only a portion of a control mark, possibly the horn and ear of a bull's head (see de Ruyter [1996] fig. 1. 339–43), is on the flan; see No. 323. Rev.: trace of control mark below horses.
325. 950.56.182   10 3.59 g (s.g. 10.587). Obv.: control symbol, dolphin (see de Ruyter [1996] fig. 1.390); see No. 323. Rev.: control mark, V. De Ruyter (1996), 130, die linkage 121.

MN.FONTEI C.F   Mint: Rome. 85 BC
Denarius. Obv.: head of Apollo r.; below, thunderbolt; behind, M·FONEI downwards; before, C·F upwards. Rev.: Cupid on goat r.; above, *pilei*; in exergue, thyrsus; around, laurel wreath. Crawford 353/1c.
326. 950.56.183   3 4.03 g. The obv. dies used for Nos. 326–28 are by Buttrey's engraver G, see Buttrey (1976) 90-3.
327. 950.56.248   12.5 3.90 g. Obv.: see No. 326. Rev.: punchmark.
328. 950.56.249   1 3.70 g. Obv.: see No. 326; die flaw across eye.

Denarius. Obv.: as above. Rev.: as above, but *pilei* on either side of goat. Crawford 353/1d.
329. 908.55.14   3 3.83 g. Obv.: from a die by Buttrey's engraver F, see Buttrey (1976) 90–93. Ex O'Hagan Collection, Sotheby (1908) lot 980.

C.LICINIVS L.F MACER   Mint: Rome. 84 BC
Denarius. Obv.: bust of Apollo seen from behind. Rev.: Minerva in quadriga r.; in exergue, C·LICINIVS·L·F . MACER Crawford 354/1.
330. 950.56.257   8 3.56 g.
331. 950.56.181   5 3.50 g (s.g. 10.804).

P.FOVRIVS CRASSIPES AED.CVR   Mint: Rome.   84 BC
(Mattingly [1982] 42, c. 85 BC)
Denarius. Obv.: head of Cybele r.; behind, AED·CVR downwards and foot turned downwards. Rev.: curule chair inscribed P·FOVRIVS   ; in exergue, CRASSIP ES . Crawford 356/1c.

    332. 969x134.67   5   3.54 g (s.g. 9.95).   Obv.: punchmark on cheek.

C.NORBANVS   Mint: Rome.   83 BC
Denarius. Obv.: head of Venus r.; behind, control mark; below, C·NORBANVS . Rev.: prow-stem, *fasces* with axe, caduceus, and ear of grain. Crawford 357/1a.

    333. 950.56.189   5   2.98 g.   Plated.   Obv.: control mark, XIIII .

        Publ.: Curry (1973) 284–85 as Sydenham 740.

Denarius. Obv.: as above. Rev.: ear of grain, *fasces* with axe, and caduceus. Crawford 357/1b.

    334. 950.56.261   7   3.81 g.   Obv.: control mark, XXVIIII .

    335. 950.56.188   7   3.48 g (s.g. 10.283).   Obv.: control mark, CXXXIIII ; from same die as Hassel (1985) taf. 22.194/4 and *BMCRR* III pl. XL.13.

L.SVLLA IMPER. ITERVM   Mint: moving with Sulla. 84–83 BC (Martin [1989] 42, after November 1, 82 BC)
Denarius. Obv.: head of Venus r.; on r., Cupid; below,   L·SVLLA . Rev.: two trophies; between, jug and *lituus*; above, IMP ER ; below, ITERV . Crawford 359/2; for a discussion of this issue, see Martin (1989) 24–44.

    336. 950.56.192   12   3.36 g (s.g. 10.23).

P.CREPVSI, C.LIMETAN, and L.CENSORIN   Mint: Rome. 82 BC
Denarius. Obv.: bust of Venus (Concordia, see Buttrey [1976] 67.n.2) r.; behind, L·CENSORIN downwards. Rev.: Victory in biga r.; above, control mark; below, C·LIMEA ; in exergue, P· CREP VSI . Crawford 360/1b.

    337. 908.55.28   7.5   3.84 g.   Obv.: from a die by engraver F, see Buttrey (1976) 90–93.   Rev.: control mark, ⅃XXXVI . Ex O'Hagan Collection, Sotheby (1908) lot 983.

P.CREPVSI   Mint: Rome. 82 BC
Denarius. Obv.: laureate head (?Apollo) r.; behind, sceptre and control letter; before, control symbol. Rev.: horseman r.; behind, control numeral; in exergue, P·CREP VSI. Crawford 361/1c. For an examination of these denarii and the engravers of the obverse dies, see Buttrey (1976).

    338. 950.56.186   2   3.92 g.   Obv.: cornucopiae and B . Rev.: CCC⅃XXXV(?). Control marks as Buttrey (1976) 78: group 19 and obverse dies of Nos. 338–39 by Buttrey's engraver G.

    339. 950.56.239 2.5 3.88 g.   From same dies as No. 338.

    340. 969x134.71   10   3.12 g.   Plated.   Obv.: control symbol off flan; control letter, A . Rev.: control numeral, illegible.

C.MAMIL LIMETANVS C.F   Mint: Rome. 82 BC
Denarius serratus. Obv.: bust of Mercury r.; behind, control letter. Rev.: Odysseus standing r., extending his hand to his dog, Argus; on l., C·MAMIL downwards; on r., LIMEⱯN upwards. Crawford 362/1.

    341. 950.56.185   8   3.49 g (s.g. 10.13).   Obv.: control letter, M as *BMCRR* I 344.2725; from a die by Buttrey's engraver G, see Buttrey (1976) 90–93. From same dies as Spink and Son (1977) 368.8141. Ex O'Hagan Collection, Sotheby (1908) lot 983.

    342. 950.56.281   2   3.89 g.   Obv.: control letter, N as *BMCRR* I 344.2726; from a die by engraver F, see Buttrey (1976) 90–93. Ex O'Hagan Collection, Sotheby (1908) lot 983.

L.CENSOR   Mint: Rome. 82 BC
Denarius. Obv.: head of Apollo r. Rev.: Marsyas walking l.; behind, column bearing statue of Victory; before, L·CENSOR downwards; on r., control mark. Crawford 363/1c.

    343. 969x134.127   2   3.31 g.   Obv.: three punchmarks. Rev.: illegible control mark.

Denarius. Obv.: as above. Rev.: as above, but no control mark. Crawford 363/1d.

    344. 950.56.187   8   4.04 g.   The obv. dies of Nos. 344–45 are by Buttrey's engraver G, see Buttrey (1976) 90–93. Ex O'Hagan Collection, Sotheby (1908) lot 983.

    345. 950.56.259   6   3.46 g (s.g. 10.37).   Obv.: see No. 344. Ex O'Hagan Collection, Sotheby (1908) lot 983.

Q.ANTO BALB PR   Mint: Rome. 83–82 BC (Mattingly [1982] 42, 82 BC)
Denarius serratus. Obv.: head of Jupiter r.; before, control mark; behind, S·C downward. Rev.: Victory in quadriga r.; in exergue,   Q·AⱯOBA.B / P R . Crawford 364/1c.

    346. 969x134.8   6   3.60 g.   Obv.: control mark, M· ; die scratched in front of face. From same dies as Owl Ltd. and McKenna (1980) pl. 8.175.

Denarius serratus. Obv.: as above, but no control mark. Rev.: as above, but below, control mark. Crawford 364/1d.

    347. 950.56.190   5   3.83 g.   Rev.: control mark, F .

Q.MAX   Mint: Rome. 82–80 BC
Denarius. Obv.: head of Apollo r.; behind, ROMA downwards; below, Q·MX or Q·MX ; before, lyre and ✳ . Rev.: cornucopiae superimposed on thunderbolt; around, wreath composed of ears of grain and assorted fruits. Crawford 371/1; for the association of this issue with Crawford 265 (No. 153), see Crawford 752 and Metcalf (1976) 215–16.

    348. 950.56.131   5   3.85 g.   Obv.: moneyer's name off flan.

A.POST A.F S.N ALBIN   Mint: Rome. 81 BC
Denarius serratus. Obv.: bust of Diana r.; above, bucranium. Rev.: lighted altar, flanked by bull and togate figure holding sprinkler (*aspergillum*), on rock; around, ᖾ , AP OST·A·F·S·N·A·BIN . Crawford 372/1.
> **349.** 908.55.37   8 3.86 g. The obv. die was cut by Buttrey's engraver F, see Buttrey (1976) 93. Ex O'Hagan Collection, Sotheby (1908) lot 985.

Denarius serratus. Obv.: head of Hispania r.; behind, HISPAN downwards. Rev.: togate figure between legionary eagle and *fasces* with axe; around, ᖽ , AP OST·A·F·S·N·A·BIN. Crawford 372/2.
> **350.** 969x134.70   3 3.82 g. Obv.: two punchmarks. The obverse dies of Nos. 350–53 were cut by Buttrey's engraver G, see Buttrey (1976) 93.
> **351.** 969x134.69   10 3.81 g. Obv.: see No. 350.
> **352.** 969x134.97   3 3.81 g. Obv.: see No. 350.
> **353.** 969x134.100   7 3.66 g (s.g. 10.401). Obv.: see No. 350.

C.MARI C.F CAPIT   Mint: Rome. 81 BC
Denarius serratus. Obv.: bust of Ceres r.; around, ᖾ , CAP IT and control numeral; below chin, control symbol. Rev.: ploughman with yoke of oxen l.; above, control numeral; in exergue, C·MARI·C·F. SC Crawford 378/1c.
> **354.** 950.56.191   5 3.56 g (s.g. 10.317). Obv.: control symbol, tall two-handled vase. Control numeral on obv. and rev., CXX as *BMCRR* I 356.2881 and Fava (1969) 53.165.

L.PROCILI F   Mint: Rome. 80 BC
Denarius. Obv.: head of Jupiter r.; behind, S·C downwards. Rev.: Juno Sospita standing r.; before, snake; behind, L·P ROCILI F downwards. Crawford 379/1.
> **355.** 950.56.266   5 3.78 g.
> **356.** 950.56.197   5 3.57 g (s.g. 10.672).
> **357.** 969x134.112   1.5 3.46 g (s.g. 10.464). Obv.: two punchmarks.
> **358.** 969x134.143   2 2.63 g. Plated.

Denarius serratus. Obv.: head of Juno Sospita r.; behind, S·C downwards. Rev.: Juno Sospita in biga r.; below, snake; in exergue, L·P ROCILI·F . Crawford 379/2.
> **359.** 987.257.42   1 2.86 g (s.g. 9.656). Broken.
> **360.** 969x134.88   5 2.43 g. Plated.
> > Publ.: Curry (1973) 284–85 as Sydenham 772.

C.POBLICI Q.F   Mint: Rome. 80 BC
Denarius serratus. Obv.: bust of Roma r.; behind, ROMA downwards; above, control mark. Rev.: Hercules strangling the Nemean lion; on r., C·P OBLICI·Q·F upwards; above, control mark. Crawford 380/1.
> **361.** 950.56.193   9 3.35 g (s.g. 10.205). Broken. Obv. and rev.: control mark, R as *BMCRR* I 366.2912.
> **362.** 950.56.263   9 3.80 g. Obv. and rev.: control mark, S as *BMCRR* I 366.2913.

C.NAE BALB   Mint: Rome. 79 BC
Denarius serratus. Obv.: head of Venus r.; behind, S·C downwards; before, control mark. Rev.: Victory in triga r.; in exergue, C·NÆ·BA·B . Crawford 382/1a.
> **363.** 969x134.37   6 3.86 g. Obv.: only part of a control letter on flan.

Denarius serratus. Obv.: as above, but no control mark. Rev.: as above, but above, control mark. Crawford 382/1b.
> **364.** 969x134.36   5 3.83 g. Rev.: control numeral, CⅬⅢ as *BMCRR* I 369.2964.

TI.CLAVD TI.F AP.N   Mint: Rome. 79 BC
Denarius serratus. Obv.: bust of Diana r.; before, S·C upwards. Rev.: Victory in biga r.; below, control mark; in exergue, TI·CLA·TI·F. A·N Crawford 383/1.
> **365.** 969x134.31   7 3.89 g. Rev.: control mark, XXⅢ within the first series.

L.PAPI   Mint: Rome. 79 BC
Denarius serratus. Obv.: head of Juno Sospita r.; behind, control mark. Rev.: gryphon leaping r.; below, control mark; in exergue, L·P AP I . Crawford 384/1.
> **366.** 950.56.194   4 3.50 g (s.g. 10.069). Obv.: control mark, beetroot or turnip; three punchmarks. Rev.: control mark, carrot. Cf. *BMCRR* I 379.3083; Sukiennik (1985) 72.262. From same dies as Fava (1969) tav.XVI.522.
> > Publ.: Curry (1973) 333–34 as Sydenham 773 but No. 366 is not plated.

M.VOLTEI M.F.   Mint: Rome. 78 BC (Hersh and Walker [1984] Table 2.6, 75 BC)
Denarius. Obv.: head of Jupiter r. Rev.: Capitoline temple; below, M·VOLTEI·M·F . Crawford 385/1.
> **367.** 950.56.195   2 4.03 g.

Denarius. Obv.: head of Liber r. Rev.: Ceres in biga of snakes r., holding torch in each hand; behind, control symbol; in exergue, M·VOLTEI·M·F . Crawford 385/3.
> **368.** 950.56.196   7 3.59 g (s.g. 10.341). Rev.: part of a control symbol on flan.

Denarius. Obv.: draped and helmeted bust r.; behind, control symbol. Rev.: Cybele in biga of lions r.; above, control numeral; in exergue, M·VOLTEI·M·F . Crawford 385/4.
> **369.** 969x134.120   5 3.51 g (s.g. 10.236). Obv.: control symbol, dividers. Rev.: control numeral, ᵶE . Cf. Crawford table XXXV. From same dies as Belloni (1977) 77:213.

L.RVTILI FLAC   Mint: Rome. 77 BC
Denarius. Obv.: head of Roma r.; behind, FLAC downwards. Rev.: Victory in biga r.; in exergue, L·RVTILI . Crawford 387/1.
> **370.** 921.62.40   9 3.35 g. Plated.

P.SATRIENVS   Mint: Rome. 77 BC
Denarius. Obv.: head of Roma r.; behind, control mark. Rev.: she-wolf l.; above, ROMA ; in exergue, P·SATRIE NVS . Crawford 388/1b.
>   **371.** 908.55.39   9   3.51 g (s.g. 10.353). Obv.: only a trace of a control mark on flan; punchmark. Ex O'Hagan Collection, Sotheby (1908) lot 986.
>   **372.** 908.55.40   7   2.92 g. Plated. Obv.: control mark, LXVI . From same dies as Calicó (1983) 239.1.243. Ex O'Hagan Collection, Sotheby (1908) lot 986.

L.RVSTI   Mint: Rome. 76 BC (Hersh and Walker [1984] Table 2.8, 74 BC)
Denarius. Obv.: head of Minerva r.; behind, S·C downwards; before, ✳ . Rev.: ram r.; in exergue, L·RVSTI . Crawford 389/1.
>   **373.** 950.56.199   7   3.52 g (s.g. 9.991). Ex O'Hagan Collection, Sotheby (1908) lot 986.

L.LVCRETI TRIO   Mint: Rome. 76 BC (Hersh and Walker [1984] Table 2.9, 74 BC)
Denarius. Obv.: head of Sol r. Rev.: crescent within seven stars; above crescent, TRIO ; below crescent, L·LVCRETI . Crawford 390/1.
>   **374.** 908.55.26   11.5   3.89 g. Ex O'Hagan Collection, Sotheby (1908) lot 983.

Denarius. Obv.: head of Neptune r.; behind, control mark. Rev.: winged boy on dolphin r.; below, L·LVCRETI TRIO . Crawford 390/2.
>   **375.** 908.55.27   2   3.29 g (s.g. 10.17). Obv.: control mark, LXIX . From the same dies as Sydenham pl. 22.784 and Berk (1988) no. 254. Ex O'Hagan Collection, Sotheby (1908) lot 983.

L.FARSVLEI MENSOR   Mint: Rome. 75 BC (Hersh and Walker [1984] Table 2.4, 76 BC)
Denarius. Obv.: bust of Libertas r.; behind, *pileus*; before, MENSOR upwards; below chin, S·C ; behind, control mark. Rev.: warrior assisting togate figure into biga; below, scorpion; in exergue, L·FARSVLEI . Crawford 392/1a.
>   **376.** 921.62.14   4   3.88 g. Obv.: illegible control mark.

CN.LEN Q   Mint: perhaps Spain. 76–75 BC
Denarius. Obv.: male bust r. (Genius populi Romani); above, G·P·R . Rev.: sceptre with wreath, globe, and rudder; on l., EX ; on r., S·C ; below, CN·LEN·Q . Crawford 393/1a.
>   **377.** 921.62.10   5.5   3.89 g.
>   **378.** 921.62.9   7   3.80 g. Rev.: from same die as No. 377.
>   **379.** 948x171.3   5   3.05 g. Plated.

C.POSTVMI AT or TA   Mint: Rome. 74 BC (Hersh and Walker [1984] Table 2.10, 73 BC)
Denarius. Obv.: bust of Diana r. Rev.: hound running r.; below, spear; in ex., C·P OSTVMI Ā Crawford 394/1a.
>   **380.** 969x134.139   7   3.87 g.
>   **381.** 950.56.198   7   3.85 g.
>   **382.** 969x134.141   6   3.82 g. Rev.: from same die as No. 383 and Berk (1986c) no. 285.

383. 969x134.140   5   3.80 g. Obv.: punchmark on cheek. Rev.: see No. 382.

MN.AQVIL MN.F MN.N   Mint: Rome. 71 BC (Hersh and Walker [1984] Table 2.21, 65 BC)
Denarius serratus. Obv.: bust of Virtus r.; before, VIRTVS upwards; behind, IIIVIR downwards. Rev.: warrior raising fallen figure; below, SICIL ; on r., MN·AQVIL upwards; on l., MN·F·MN·N downwards. Crawford 401/1.
>   **384.** 908.55.2   6   3.95 g (s.g. 9.952). From same dies as Malloy (1978) lot 641. Ex O'Hagan Collection, Sotheby (1908) lot 977.
>   **385.** 908.55.1   5   3.37 g (s.g. 9.875). Ex O'Hagan Collection, Sotheby (1908) lot 977.

KALENI, CORDI   Mint: Rome. 70 BC (Hersh and Walker [1984] Table 2.18, 68 BC)
Denarius serratus. Obv.: jugate heads of Honos and Virtus r.; on l., HO ; on r., VIR ; below, KALENI . Rev.: Italia and Roma clasping hands; between, cornucopiae; on l., caduceus and IA ; on r., RO ; in exergue, CORDI . Crawford 403/1.
>   **386.** 921.62.15   5   3.95 g.
>   **387.** 912x17.47   3   3.78 g.

M.PLAETORIVS CEST   Mint: Rome. 69 BC (Mattingly [1982] 45, ?73 BC; Hersh and Walker [1984] Table 2.34, 57 BC)
Denarius. Obv.: female bust (Proserpina) r.; behind, control mark. Rev.: winged caduceus; on r., M·P·LAETORI downwards; on l., CEST·EX·S·C downwards. Crawford 405/3b.
>   **388.** 950.56.201   6   3.44 g (s.g. 10.147). Obv.: control mark, vase with strap (*BMCRR* I [repr., 1970] x.3541). From same dies as Calicó (1983) 213.1.108, Auctiones (1975) 30.390, and Münzen und Medaillen (1984) pl. 26.388.

Denarius. Obv.: as above. Rev.: jug and torch; on r., M·P·LAETORI downwards; on l., CEST·EX·S·C downwards. Crawford 405/4b.
>   **389.** 950.56.229   7   4.04 g. Obv.: control mark, butterfly as listed by Crawford Table XLI.4b and Fava (1969) tav. P.547; from same die as Calicó (1983) 214.1.111 and Levy and Bastien I (1985) pl. V.380. Ratto (1928) lot 1367.

P.GALB AED. CVR   Mint: Rome. 69 BC
Denarius. Obv.: head of Vesta r.; behind, S·C downwards. Rev.: knife, *cullullus* and axe; on l., AE ; on r., CVR ; in exergue, P·GALB . Crawford 406/1.
>   **390.** 921.62.49   5   4.15 g. Obv.: curved incisions in field at r. Rev.: dot at centre as on Crawford pl. L.14, Sydenham pl. 24.839, Hassel (1985) 25.228, and Herbert (1987) pl. 20.555.

C.HOSIDI C.F GETA III VIR   Mint: Rome. 68 BC (Hersh and Walker [1984] Table 2.22, 64 BC)
Denarius serratus. Obv.: bust of Diana r.; behind, GETA downwards; before, III·VIR downwards. Rev.: wounded boar r., attacked by hound; in exergue, C·HOSIDI·C·F . Crawford 407/1.

391. 908.55.17   3 3.72 g. Obv.: from same die as Münzen und Medaillen (1975) pl. 24.397 and Berk (1986a) no. 237. Ex O'Hagan Collection, Sotheby (1908) lot 981.

C.PISO L.F. FRVGI   Mint: Rome. 67 BC (Hersh and Walker [1984] Table 2.27, 61 BC)
Denarius. Obv.: head of Apollo r.; behind, control mark. Rev.: horseman galloping r.; below, variations of the moneyer's name; above, control mark. Crawford 408/1a.

392. 950.56.203   6 4.00 g. Obv.: control mark, ✳ . Rev.: C·P IS·L·F·FRVGI ; control symbol, vertical club. Crawford, Table XLII: obv. die 43 and rev. die 48; Hersh (1976) 33.90 (O-34 and R-1039). From same dies as Belloni (1960) tav. 46.1722. Ratto (1928) lot 983.

393. 950.56.235   5 3.85 g. Obv.: control mark, I . Rev.: C·P ISO·L·F·FRVGI; control symbol, stalk(?). Crawford, Table XLII: obv. die 47 and rev. die 54; Hersh (1976) 33.95 (O-36 and R-1053).

Denarius. Obv.: head of Apollo r. or l.; behind, control mark. Rev.: as above, but with or without palm. Crawford 408/1b.

394. 950.56.208   7 3.73 g. Obv.: head r.; control mark, III⁼ . Rev.: palm tied with fillet; C·P ISO·L·F·FRVG ; control mark, ⇀ . Crawford, Table XLIII: obv. die 38 and rev. die 52 but with FRV; Hersh (1976) 36.134 (O-201 and R-2004). The same obv. die is linked with Hersh (1976) 23.R-2028 on Berk (1986a) no. 230.

395. 950.56.236   6 3.54 g (s.g. 10.473). Obv.: head l.; control mark, IS⋮ ; from same die as Auctiones (1986) 31.356 and Sotheby (1983) lot. 210. Rev.: no palm; C·P ISOLFFRV(G) ; control mark, ·I . Crawford, Table XLIII: obv. die 47 and rev. die 51; Hersh (1976) 56.438 (O-801 and R-2005). Four denarii from these dies occurred in the Mesagne Hoard, see Hersh and Walker (1984) 123.89.

396. 969x134.23   6 3.88 g. Obv.: head r.; control symbol, lizard. Rev.: no palm; C·P ISOLFFRVG ; control mark, Λ ; from same die as *NFA* (1981) lot 277. From same dies as Münzen und Medaillen (1989) 4.52. Crawford, Table XLIII: obv. die 48 and rev. die 53; Hersh (1976) 36.144 (O-203 and R-2008).

397. 969x134.24   6 3.90 g. Obv.: head r.; control mark, I⁚ ; two punchmarks. Rev.: no palm; C·P ISOLFFRV; control mark, O . Crawford, Table XLIII: obv. die 63 and rev. die 85; Hersh (1976) 39.188 (O-217 and R-2029).

M.PLAETORIUS M.F CESTIANVS AED.CVR   Mint: Rome. 67 BC
Denarius. Obv.: bust r., with attributes of Isis, Minerva, Apollo, Diana, and Victory; before, cornucopiae; behind, CESTIANVS downwards; before, S·C downwards. Rev.: eagle on thunderbolt; around ꓶ M·P LAETORIVS·M·F·AED·CVR . Crawford 409/1.

398. 921.62.28   5 3.43 g (s.g. 10.482). Obv.: two punchmarks. From same dies as Schulman (1966) pl. 12.1447.

399. 921.62.27   4 3.38 g (s.g. 10.396).

Denarius. Obv.: head of Cybele r.; behind, forepart of lion; before, globe; behind, CESTIANVS downwards. Rev.: curule chair; on l., control mark; around ꓶ , M·P LAETORIVS·AED·CVR·EX·S·C . Crawford 409/2.

400. 969x134.44   6 3.66 g (s.g. 10.431). Rev.: control mark, ship's stern.

Q.POMPONI MVSA   Mint: Rome. 66 BC (Hersh and Walker [1984] Table 2.40, 56 BC)
Denarius. Obv.: head of Apollo r.; behind, scroll. Rev.: Clio l., holding scroll; on r., Q·P OMP ONI downwards; on l., MVSA downwards. Crawford 410/3.

401. 908.55.34   5 3.13 g (s.g. 9.965). Broken. Obv.: from same die as Münzen und Medaillen (1970) pl. 12.140. Ex O'Hagan Collection, Sotheby (1908) lot 985.

Denarius. Obv.: as above, but behind, sandal. Rev.: Thalia l., holding comic mask; on r., Q·P OMP ONI downwards; on l., MVSA downwards. Crawford 410/9b.

402. 908.55.35   12 3.60 g (s.g. 10.23). Rev.: from same die as Bank Leu (1977) taf. XXIV.564, Auctiones (1979) 29.397, and Calicó (1983) 227.1.192. Ex O'Hagan Collection, Sotheby (1908) lot 985.

Denarius. Obv.: as above, but behind, wreath. Rev.: Polyhymnia wearing wreath; on r., Q·P OMP ONI downwards; on l., MVSA downwards. Crawford 410/10a.

403. 950.56.230   5 3.86 g. From same dies as Münzen und Medaillen (1970) pl. 12.142. Ex O'Hagan Collection, Sotheby (1908) lot 985.

L.ROSCI FABATI   Mint: Rome. 64 BC (Hersh and Walker [1984] Table 2.29, 59 BC)
Denarius serratus. Obv.: head of Juno Sospita r.; behind, control mark; below, L·ROSCI . Rev.: girl and snake; on l., control mark; in exergue, FABATI . Crawford 412/1.

404. 969x134.146   5 3.94 g. For the control symbols on the obv. and rev., see Crawford pl. LXIX.168 but the shape of the control symbol on the rev. is much clearer on No. 404.

405. 969x134.147   6 3.79 g. Obv.: control mark, dice box; two punchmarks. Rev.: control mark, two flutes; punchmark. Control marks as Crawford, pl. LXVIII.34.

L.CASSI LONGIN   Mint: Rome. 63 BC (Mattingly [1982] 45, ?58 BC); Hersh and Walker [1984] Table 2.28, 60 BC)
Denarius. Obv.: head of Vesta l.; on r., dish; on l., control letter. Rev.: voter dropping tablet marked V into *cista*; on r., LONGIN·III·V downwards. Crawford 413/1.

406. 969x134.27   6 3.87 g. Obv.: control letter, A as Hersh and Walker (1984) 128.413/1.1.

L.FVRI CN.F BROCCHI   Mint: Rome. 63 BC
Denarius. Obv.: head of Ceres r., flanked by ear of grain and kernel of barley; on either side, III VIR ; below, BROCCHI .

Rev.: curule chair between two *fasces*; above, L·FV̀RI . CN·F Crawford 414/1.

407. 921.62.18   6 3.87 g. Rev.: from same die as *NFA* (1979) lot 503.
408. 921.62.16   5 3.86 g.
409. 921.62.17   7 3.76 g.

LIBO   Mint: Rome. 62 BC
Denarius. Obv.: head of Bonus Eventus r.; behind, LIBO downwards; before, BON·EVENT downwards. Rev.: Puteal Scribonianum; at base, hammer; above, P·VTEAL ; below, SCRIBON . Crawford 416/1a.

410. 921.62.43   5.5 4.00 g. From same dies as Berk (1986a) no. 250.
411. 921.62.44   7 3.54 g.
412. 921.62.42   5.5 3.60 g.
413. 921.62.45   5.5 3.39 g (s.g. 10.328). Obv.: two punchmarks. Rev.: punchmark.

P.YPSAE   Mint: Rome. 60 BC (Mattingly [1982] 45, ?66 BC; Hersh and Walker [1984] Table 2.37, 57 BC)
Denarius. Obv.: head of Neptune r.; behind, trident; before, P·YP·SAE·S·C downwards. Rev.: Jupiter in quadriga l.; below, C·YP·SAE·COS / P·RIV ; behind, CEP·IT upwards. Crawford 420/1a.

414. 908.55.32   4 3.93 g. Obv.: traces of two punchmarks. Ex O'Hagan Collection, Sotheby (1908) lot 985.

Denarius. Obv.: bust of Leuconoe r.; behind, dolphin; before, P·YP·SAE·S·C downwards. Rev.: as above. Crawford 420/2a.

415. 950.56.204   5 3.98 g. Obv.: single necklace. Rev.: from same die as Münzen und Medaillen (1982) 41.319. From same dies as *NS* (1977) 10.70. Ratto (1927) lot 1376.
416. 908.55.33   6 3.75 g. Obv.: double necklace. Rev.: from same die as Herbert (1987) pl. 21.593. Ex O'Hagan Collection, Sotheby (1908) lot 985.
417. 969x134.126   11 2.38 g. Plated. Obv: details illegible. Not illustrated.

M.SCAVR, P.HVPSAEVS AED. CVR   Mint: Rome. 58 BC
Denarius. Obv: kneeling Aretas r., with camel; above, M·SCAVR / AED·CVR ; at sides, EX S·C ; in ex., REX·ARETAS . Rev.: Jupiter in quadriga l.; below horses, scorpion; above, P·HVP·SAE / AED·CVR ; below, C·HVP·SAE·COS / P·REIVE ; on r., CAP·T upwards. Crawford 422/1b.

418. 969x134.125   5 3.68 g. Rev.: legend as *BMCRR* I 484.3881.

C.CONSIDI NONIANI   Mint: Rome. 57 BC (Hersh and Walker [1984] Table 2.41, 56 BC)
Denarius. Obv.: bust of Venus r.; behind, C·CONSIDI·NONIANI downwards; before, S·C upwards. Rev.: temple on mountain, surrounded by wall with gate; above gate, ERVC . Crawford 424/1.

419. 950.56.206   5 2.94 g (s.g. 10.176). Broken.

PHILIPPVS   Mint: Rome. 56 BC (Hersh and Walker [1984] Table 2.36, 57 BC)
Denarius. Obv.: head of Ancus Marcius r.; behind, *lituus*; below, ANCVS . Rev.: equestrian statue and flower on aqueduct; on l., P·HILIP·P·VS downwards; within arches, AQVA·MR . Crawford 425/1.

420. 969x134.109   4 4.00 g.
421. 969x134.110   5 4.00 g.
422. 908.55.29   5.5 3.94 g. Rev.: AQVA·MRC . Ex O'Hagan Collection, Sotheby (1908) lot 983.
423. 969x134.108   10 3.86 g.
424. 969x134.111   5 3.81 g.
425. 921.62.25   5 3.72 g.

FAVSTVS   Mint: Rome. 56 BC
Denarius. Obv.: bust of Venus r.; behind, sceptre and S·C downwards. Rev.: three trophies between jug and *lituus*; in exergue, ᴧ·A᷍. Crawford 426/3.

426. 950.56.214   3 4.09 g. Ratto (1927) lot 1086.
427. 969x134.166   2 4.01 g.

Denarius. Obv.: head of Hercules r.; on l., S·C downwards. Rev.: globe surrounded by three small wreaths and one large wreath (the three triumphs of Pompey and the *corona aurea* granted to him in 63); below, aplustre and ear of grain. Crawford 426/4b.

428. 921.62.11   8 3.82 g. Rev.: from same die as Niggeler (1966) taf. 19.868.

C.MEMMI C.F   Mint: Rome. 56 BC
Denarius. Obv.: head of Ceres r.; before, C·MEMMI·C·F downwards. Rev.: trophy and kneeling captive; on r., C·MEMMIVS downwards; on l., IMP·ERATOR downwards. Crawford 427/1.

429. 950.56.260   1 3.02 g. Plated. Ex O'Hagan Collection, Sotheby (1908) lot 983.
Publ.: Curry (1973) 284–5 as Sydenham 920.

Denarius. Obv.: head of Quirinus r.; behind, Q·VIRINVS downwards; before, C·MEMMI·C·F downwards. Rev.: Ceres seated r.; before, snake; around ᴖ , MEMMIVS·AED· CERIALIA·P·REIMVS·FECIT . Crawford 427/2.

430. 969x134.113   9 3.60 g. Holed.

Q.CASSIVS   Mint: Rome. 55 BC
Denarius. Obv.: head of Genius populi Romani r. Rev.: eagle on thunderbolt r., between *lituus* and jug; below, Q·CASSIVS . Crawford 428/3.

431. 950.56.212 6 3.75 g.
432. 969x134.30   5 3.52 g (s.g. 10.099).
433. 969x134.49   10 3.22 g. Broken.

P.FONTEIVS P.F CAPITO   Mint: Rome. 55 BC
Denarius. Obv.: bust of Mars r.; on r., P·FONTEIVS·P·F downwards; on l., CAP·ITO·III·VIR upwards. Rev.: horseman r., spearing warrior who is about to stab a captive; on r., helmet and shield; above, M·FON·TR·MIL . Crawford 429/1.

434. 950.56.211   5 3.96 g. Short diagonal incision across centre of obv. and rev. From same dies as Münzen und Medaillen (1973) 7.39. Ex O'Hagan Collection, Sotheby (1908) lot 980.

Denarius. Obv.: head of Concordia r.; around Ω , P·FONT(or N)EIVS·CAPITO·III·VIR·CONCORDIA . Rev.: Villa Publica; on l., T·DIDI downwards; below, IMP ; on r., VIL·P·VB upwards. Crawford 429/2a.

435. 950.56.251 2 3.86 g. Die flaws on obv. and rev.

P.CRASSVS M.F   Mint: Rome. 55 BC

Denarius. Obv.: bust of Venus r.; behind, S·C downwards. Rev.: female figure leading horse l.; at feet, cuirass and shield; at l., P·CRASSVS upwards; at r., M·F downwards. Crawford 430/1.

436. 950.56.213 1 4.17 g. From same dies as Münzen und Medaillen (1975) pl. 24.412. Ratto (1928) lot 1223.
437. 969x134.79 3 3.51 g (s.g. 10.309).
438. 969x134.78 11 2.41 g. Plated. Obv.: three punchmarks. Rev.: punchmark.

A.PLAVTIVS AED.CVR   Mint: Rome. 55 BC

Denarius. Obv.: head of Cybele r.; before, A·P·LAVTIVS downwards; behind, AED·CVR·S·C downwards. Rev.: kneeling figure r. with camel; in exergue, BACCHIVS ; before, IVDAEVS upwards. Crawford 431/1.

439. 921.62.30 9 4.31 g.
440. 921.62.31 5 3.87 g.
441. 921.62.29 1 3.82 g.
442. 969x134.131 5 3.63 g (s.g. 9.97).

BRVTVS   Mint: Rome. 54 BC

Denarius. Obv.: head of Libertas r.; behind, LIBERTAS downwards. Rev.: L. Iunius Brutus, Cos. 509, between two lictors, preceded by an *accensus*; in exergue, BRVTVS . Crawford 433/1.

443. 950.56.210 6 3.82 g. Rev.: from same die as Galerie des Monnaies of Geneva Ltd. (1978) no. 1588 and Berk (1988) no. 262.

Denarius. Obv.: head of L. Iunius Brutus, Cos. 509, r.; behind, BRVTVS downwards. Rev.: head of C. Servilius Ahala, Mag. Eq. 439, r.; behind, AHALA downwards. Crawford 433/2.

444. 950.56.209 4.5 3.64 g (s.g. 10.511). Obv.: from same die as Auctiones (1983) 39.564.

CALDVS IIIVIR   Mint: Rome. 51 BC (Hersh and Walker [1984] Table 2.51, 53 BC)

Denarius. Obv.: head of C. Coelius Caldus, Cos. 94, r.; before, C·COEL·CALDVS downwards; below, COS ; behind, tablet inscribed L·D . Rev.: head of Sol r., between oval shield and Macedonian shield; before, CALDVS·III·VIR downwards. Crawford 437/1a.

445. 950.56.207 8 3.59 g (s.g. 10.418). Obv.: from same die as Auctiones (1988) taf. 21.471. Rev.: die flaw in radiate crown.

MN.ACILIVS IIIVIR   Mint: Rome. 49 BC

Denarius. Obv.: head of Salus r.; behind, SALVTIS down

wards. Rev.: Valetudo standing l.; on r., M·ACILIVS downwards; on l., III·VIR·VALEV upwards. Crawford 442/1b.

446. 950.164.19 2 3.05 g.

CAESAR   Mint: moving with Caesar. 49–48 BC

Denarius. Obv.: priestly implements. Rev.: elephant r., trampling dragon; in exergue, CAESAR . Crawford 443/1.

447. 950.56.216 2 3.96 g.
448. 969x134.156 5 3.47 g (s.g. 10.345).

L.HOSTILIVS SASERNA   Mint: Rome. 48 BC

Denarius. Obv.: female head r. Rev.: Victory walking r.; before, L·HOSTILIVS downwards; behind, SASERNA upwards. Crawford 448/1a.

449. 908.55.25 10 3.67 g (s.g. 10.332). Ex O'Hagan Collection, Sotheby (1908) lot 981.
450. 908.55.24 5 3.27 g (s.g. 9.788). Ex O'Hagan Collection, Sotheby (1908) lot 981.

Denarius. Obv.: male bust r.; behind, Gallic shield. Rev.: warrior and charioteer in biga r.; above, L·HOSTILIVS ; below, SASERN . Crawford 448/2a.

451. 908.55.20 5 2.91 g. Plated. Ex O'Hagan Collection, Sotheby (1908) lot 981.

Denarius. Obv.: female head r.; behind, *carnyx*. Rev.: Artemis of Massalia and stag; on r., L·HOSTILIVS downwards; on l., SASERNA upwards. Crawford 448/3.

452. 908.55.22 10 4.33 g. Ex O'Hagan Collection, Sotheby (1908) lot 981.
453. 908.55.23 7 3.75 g. Ex O'Hagan Collection, Sotheby (1908) lot 981.
454. 908.55.21 3 3.63 g (s.g. 10.245). From same dies as Gorini (1973) 78.426. Ex O'Hagan Collection, Sotheby (1908) lot 981.

C.VIBIVS C.F C.N PANSA   Mint: Rome. 48 BC

Denarius. Obv.: mask of Pan r.; below, PANSA . Rev.: Jupiter A(n)xurus seated l.; on r., C·VIBIVS·C·F·C·N downwards; on l., IOVIS·AXVR upwards. Crawford 449/1a.

455. 921.62.54 5 3.51 g (s.g. 10.199). Rev.: punch mark.

Denarius. Obv.: head of Liber r.; behind, PANSA downwards. Rev.: Ceres walking r.; before, plough; on l., C·VIBIVS·C·F·C·N downwards. Crawford 449/2.

456. 969x134.119 5 3.51 g (s.g. 10.193).

ALBINVS BRVTI.F   Mint: Rome. 48 BC

Denarius. Obv.: head of Pietas r.; behind, PIETAS downwards. Rev.: two hands clasped around caduceus; below, ALBINVS·BRVTI·F . Crawford 450/2.

457. 921.62.36 5.5 3.72 g.
458. 921.62.37 5.5 3.66 g. Obv.: from same die as Berk (1986b) no. 193 and Auctiones (1988) 37.479.

Denarius. Obv.: head of A. Postumius r.; around ☉ , A·P·OSTVMIVS·COS . Rev.: wreath of ears of grain; within, ALBINV BRVTI·F . Crawford 450/3a.

    459. 921.62.38 5 3.65 g. Rev.: dot at centre as on Ratto (1928) pl. XVII:1453.

Denarius. Obv.: as above. Rev.: as above but within wreath, ALBINV BRVTI·F . Crawford 450/3b.

    460. 921.62.39 10 3.69 g. Obv.: from same die as Berk (1986c) no. 296. From same dies as Münzen und Medaillen (1975) pl. 25.420 and Münzen und Medaillen (1982) 42.338.

CAESAR   Mint: moving with Caesar. 13 July 48–47 BC

Denarius. Obv.: female head r.; behind, ⊥II downwards. Rev.: trophy with Gallic shield and *carnyx*; on r., axe; below, CAE SAR . Crawford 452/2.

    461. 950.56.217 7 4.02 g. Obv.: from same die as Bank Leu (1987) 32.211.

    462. 969x134.157 3 3.65 g (s.g. 10.298).

L.PLAVTIVS PLANCVS   Mint: Rome. 47 BC

Denarius. Obv.: head of Medusa facing; below, L·P·LAVTIVS . Rev.: Victory leading four horses; below, P·LANCVS . Crawford 453/1a.

    463. 921.62.32 8 3.97 g.

    464. 969x134.130 6 3.14 g (s.g. 9.978).

    465. 921.62.33 5 2.87 g. Plated.

        Publ.: Curry (1973) 284–5 as Sydenham 959.

A.LICINIVS NERVA IIIVIR   Mint: Rome. 47 BC

Denarius. Obv.: head of Fides r.; before, FIDES downwards; behind, NERVA downwards. Rev.: horseman dragging naked warrior; below, A·LICINIVS ; in field, III VIR . Crawford 454/1.

    466. 950.56.219 9 3.81 g. Rev.: l. arm of horseman is missing; from same die as Superior (1988) 145.1728. Ratto (1928) lot 1226.

CAESAR   Mint: Africa. 47–46 BC

Denarius. Obv.: head of Venus r. Rev.: Aeneas l., carrying *palladium* and Anchises; on r., CAESAR downwards. Crawford 458/1.

    467. 950.56.279 6.5 3.88 g.

    468. 950x24.2 6 3.85 g.

    469. 950.56.218 6 3.83 g.

Q.METEL.PIVS SCIPIO IMP   Mint: Africa. 47–46 BC

Denarius. Obv.: head of Jupiter r.; before, Q·METEL downwards; below, P·IVS . Rev.: elephant r.; above, SCIPIO ; below, IMP . Crawford 459/1.

    470. 928.1.21 10 3.81 g. Rev.: die flaw between front and back legs.

    471. 912x17.48 9 3.80 g.

Q.METELL.SCIPIO IMP with EPPIVS LEG.F.C   Mint: Africa. 47–46 BC

Denarius. Obv.: head of Africa r.; on r., ear of grain; below, plough; on far r., Q·METELL downwards; on l., SCIPIO·IMP upwards. Rev.: Hercules standing facing; on r., EPPIVS downwards; on l., LEG·F·C upwards. Crawford 461/1.

    472. 950.56.220 10.5 3.42 g (s.g. 10.325). Ex O'Hagan Collection, Sotheby (1908) lot 977.

MN.CORDIVS RVFVS IIIVIR   Mint: Rome. 46 BC

Denarius. Obv.: jugate heads of Dioscuri r.; behind, RVFVS·IIIVIR downwards. Rev.: Venus standing l., with Cupid on shoulder; behind, MN·CORDI downwards. Crawford 463/1b.

    473. 950.56.221 8 3.93 g.

    474. 921.62.6 2 3.24 g (10.224). Obv.: die flaws in legend; two small incisions.

Denarius. Obv.: owl on Corinthian helmet; on l., RVFVS upwards. Rev.: *aegis* decorated with head of Medusa; around ☉ , MN·CORDIVS . Crawford 463/2.

    475. 921.62.8 2 3.37 g (s.g. 10.151). Obv.: small incisions.

Denarius. Obv.: head of Venus r.; behind, RVFVS·S·C downwards. Rev.: Cupid on dolphin; below, MN·CORDIVS . Crawford 463/3.

    476. 921.62.7 1 3.32 g (s.g. 10.461).

T.CARISIVS IIIVIR   Mint: Rome. 46 BC

Denarius. Obv.: head of Sibyl r. Rev.: sphinx r.; above head, T·CARISIVS ; in exergue, III·VIR . Crawford 464/1.

    477. 969x134.25 4.5 3.68 g (s.g. 10.381). Obv.: punch-mark.

    478. 969x134.26 7.5 3.52 g (s.g. 10.318).

Denarius. Obv.: head of Juno Moneta r.; behind, MONETA downwards. Rev.: anvil die with garlanded punch die above, flanked by tongs and hammer; above, T·CARISIVS . Crawford 464/2.

    479. 912x17.50 7 3.94 g. Obv.: from same die as Depeyrot (1985) pl.31.26; scratch from nose to edge of flan.

    480. 969x134.28 3 3.79 g. Obv.: die flaw in field.

Denarius. Obv.: head of Roma r.; behind, ROMA downwards. Rev.: cornucopiae on globe, between sceptre and rudder; below, T·CARISI . Crawford 464/3a.

    481. 908.55.7 3 4.00 g. Ex O'Hagan Collection, Sotheby (1908) lot 978.

Denarius. Obv.: bust of Victory r.; behind, S·C downwards. Rev.: Victory in quadriga r.; in exergue, T·CARISI . Crawford 464/5.

    482. 908.55.5 6.5 3.82 g. Ex O'Hagan Collection, Sotheby (1908) lot 978.

    483. 908.55.6 3 3.63 g. Ex O'Hagan Collection, Sotheby (1908) lot 978.

C.CONSIDIVS PAETVS   Mint: Rome. 46 BC
>Denarius. Obv.: head of Apollo r. Rev.: curule chair with wreath on seat; above, C·CONSIDIVS ; in exergue, P·AETVS . Crawford 465/1b.
>>**484.** 921.62.4 6 3.89 g.

>Denarius. Obv.: bust of Minerva r. Rev.: Victory in quadriga r.; in exergue, C·CONSIDI . Crawford 465/5.
>>**485.** 921.62.5 1.5 3.65 g (s.g. 10.015).

A.HIRTIVS PR, C.CAESAR COS.TER   Mint: Rome. 46 BC
>Aureus. Obv.: veiled female head r.; behind, C·CAESAR upwards; before, COS·TER downwards. Rev.: *lituus*, jug and axe; on l., A·HIRTIVS·P R downwards. Crawford 466/1; Banti and Simonetti I (1972) 33-35.tipo V, var. A.
>>**486.** 934.80.1 9 7.95 g.

COS.TERT.DICT.ITER. AVGVR PONT.MAX   Mint: uncertain. 46 BC
>Denarius. Obv.: head of Ceres r.; behind, COS·TER downwards; before, DICT·ITER upwards. Rev.: *culullus*, *aspergillum*, jug, and *lituus*; above, AVGVR ; below, P·ONT·MAX ; on r., D . Crawford 467/1a.
>>**487.** 969x134.133 1 3.84 g. Obv.: punchmark.
>>**488.** 969x134.134 12 3.91 g. Rev.: Crawford 467/1a or 1b but letter in field is off flan.

CAESAR   Mint: Spain. 46–45 BC
>Denarius. Obv.: head of Venus r.; behind, Cupid. Rev.: trophy between seated female and male captives; in exergue, CAESAR . Crawford 468/1.
>>**489.** 912x17.46 6.5 4.02 g.

>Denarius. Obv.: bust of Venus l., with Cupid on shoulder; behind, sceptre; on l., *lituus*. Rev.: trophy between kneeling male and seated female captives; in exergue, CAESAR . Crawford 468/2.
>>**490.** 969x134.135 1.5 2.96 Plated.

CN.MAGNVS IMP, M.POBLICI.LEG.PROPR   Mint: Spain. 46–45 BC
>Denarius. Obv.: head of Roma r.; before, M·P OBLICI·LEG·P RO upwards; behind, P R downwards. Rev.: female figure giving palm branch to soldier; on r., CN·MAGNVS·IMP upwards. Crawford 469/1a.
>>**491.** 969x134.137 6 3.75 g.

>Denarius. Obv.: as above. Rev.: as above, but prow of ship much larger and palm branch with long stalk. Crawford 469/1d.
>>**492.** 969x134.136 7.5 3.69 g. From same dies as Banti and Simonetti I (1972) 6.6.

L.VALERIVS ACISCVLVS   Mint: Rome. 45 BC
>Denarius. Obv.: head of Apollo r.; above, star; behind, *acisculus* and ᴗ , ACISCILVS . Rev.: Europa on bull r.; in exergue, L·VALERIVS . Crawford 474/1a-b.
>>**493.** 950.56.223 1 3.93 g. Partial brockage. Obv.: from same die as Münzen und Medaillen (1982) 44.362.

C.CLOVI.PRAEF, CAESAR DIC.TER   Mint: uncertain. 45 BC
>Orichalcum: denomination, uncertain (dupondius?, Sydenham 1025–6 and Burnett [1982] 131; equalling at least a dupondius, Crawford 573; as, Kent [1978] 273.91). Obv.: bust of Victory r.; before, CAESAR·DIC·TER upwards. Rev.: Minerva standing l.; before, snake; on l., C·CLOVI downwards; on r., P RAEF upwards. Crawford 476/1a; Banti and Simonetti I (1972) 122–24.
>>**494.** 921.6.12 12 12.02 g.

MAGNVS PIVS IMP   Mint: Spain and Sicily. 45 BC onwards
>As. Obv.: head of Janus, with features of Cn. Pompeius Magnus; above, MAGNVS or var. Rev.: prow r.; above, P IVS ; below, IMP . Crawford 479/1; for differing views on which issues were Spanish, see Morawiecki (1983) 62 and Buttrey (1989) 153.692.
>>**495.** 912x17.1 11 15.28 g. Obv.: MGN or MGN; the features are similar to Martini (1988) tav.XIII.93 and 98 (emisson [B] from an uncertain Sicilian mint).

P.ACCOLEIVS LARISCOLVS   Mint: Rome. 43 BC
>Denarius. Obv.: bust of Diana Nemorensis r.; behind, P·ACCOLEIVS upwards; before, LARISCOLVS downwards. Rev.: triple cult statue of Diana Nemorensis before cypress grove. Crawford 486/1.
>>**496.** 991.219.35 7 3.17 g. Obv.: the hairstyle belongs to Alföldi's third variety (see Alföldi [1960] 138; reference from B. R. Brace, pers. comm., 1992)

PETILLIVS CAPITOLINVS   Mint: Rome. 43 BC
>Denarius. Obv.: eagle on thunderbolt ; above, P ETILLIVS ; below, CAP ITOLINVS . Rev.: Capitoline temple; on l., F ; on r., S . Crawford 487/2c.
>>**497.** 969x134.42 4.5 3.47 g (s.g. 10.254).

M.ANTONI, in part with M.LEPID   Mint: Lugdunum. 43–42 BC
>Quinarius. Obv.: bust of Victory r. Rev.: lion r.; on l., A ; on r., XL ; above, LVGV ; below, INΛD . Crawford 489/5.
>>**498.** 989.296.2 12 1.55 g.

L.LIVINEIVS REGVLVS IIIIVIR A.P.F   Mint: Rome. 42 BC
P.CLODIVS M.F IIIIVIR A.P.F
L.MVSSIDIVS T.F LONGVS IIIIVIR A.P.F
C.V(E)IBIVS V(A)RVS
>Denarius. Obv.: head of Sol r.; behind, quiver. Rev.: crescent surrounded by five stars; below, P·CLODIVS . Crawford 494/21.
>>**499.** 950.56.225 4.5 2.65 g. Plated.
>>Publ.: Curry (1973) 284–85 as Sydenham 1115.

>Denarius. Obv.: head of Apollo r.; behind, lyre. Rev.: Diana standing facing, holding two lighted torches; on r., P·CLODIVS downwards; on l., M·F downwards. Crawford 494/23.
>>**500.** 969x134.34 3.5 3.91 g.
>>**501.** 921.62.1 1 3.77 g. Rev.: on l., ·M·F· .
>>**502.** 969x134.33 11 3.74 g. Obv.: from same die as Schulman (1974) pl. 28.1531. Rev.: on l., M·F .
>>**503.** 969x134.35 10 3.26 g (s.g. 10.02). Rev.: on l., ·M·F· .

Denarius. Obv.: head of L. Regulus, Pr., r. Rev.: modius between ears of grain; above, L·LIVINEIVS ; in exergue, REGVLVS . Crawford 494/29.

    504. 921.62.20 1.5 3.47 g (s.g. 10.573). Obv.: die flaws in field; punchmark.

Denarius. Obv.: bust of Minerva r. Rev.: Hercules standing facing; on r., C·VIBIVS downwards; on l., VARVS downwards. Crawford 494/38.

    505. 969x134.121 11 3.35 g (s.g. 9.495). Surface loss.

MAG.PIVS IMP.ITER. PRAEF.CLAS. ET ORAE MARIT   Mint: Sicily. 42-40 BC (for a date of late summer to September 36 BC, see Evans [1987] 129)

    Denarius. Obv.: head of Cn. Pompeius Magnus r.; behind, jug; before, *lituus*; around ◯ , MAG·P IVS·IMP·ITER . Rev.: Neptune standing l., between the Catanaean brothers; above, P RAEF ; in exergue, CLAS·ET·ORÆ MRIT·EX·S·C . Crawford 511/3a; for a study of this issue, see Evans (1987) 114–19.

    506. 950.56.224 12 3.83 g.

M.ANT.IMP.AVG.IIIVIR   Mint: moving with M. Antonius. 41 BC R.P.C. with M.BARBAT.Q.P,
M.NERVA PROQ.P, L.GELL.Q.P

    Denarius. Obv.: head of M. Antonius r.; around ◯ , M·ANT·IM·A/G·III·VIR·R·P ·C·M·BARBAT·Q·P . Rev.: head of Octavian r.; around ◯ , CAESAR·IMP·P ONT·III·VIR·R·P ·C . Crawford 517/2.

    507. 969x134.132 12 3.86 g.

Q.VOCONIVS VITVLVS Q.DESIGN   Mint: Rome. ?40 BC or later.

    Denarius. Obv.: head of Caesar r. Rev.: calf l.; above, Q·VOCONIVS ; in exergue, VITVLVS·Q DESIGN ; on either side, S and C . Crawford 526/4.

    508. 924.3.147 11 3.61 g.

C.CAESAR IMP, M.ANTONIVS IMP   Mint: moving with Octavian (Italy, cf. Crawford [1984] 42.201). 39 BC

    Quinarius. Obv.: head of Concordia r.; around ◡, III·VIR·R·P ·C . Rev.: two hands clasped around caduceus; around ◯, M·ANTON·C·CAESAR . Crawford 529/4b.

    509. 908.55.41 4 1.68 g. Obv.: several punchmarks. Ex O'Hagan Collection, Sotheby (1908) lot 977.

CAESAR DIVI.F   Mint: Italy. ?38 BC or later.

    Sestertius(?). Obv.: head of Octavian r.; before, CAESAR downwards; behind, DIVI·F downwards. Rev.: head of Caesar r.; before, DIVOS downwards; behind, IVLIVS downwards. Crawford 535/1; 41–0 BC, Alföldi and Giard (1984) 152; for a recent review of various dates and mints that have postulated for this issue, see Martini (1988a) 39–42, where he suggests that it was struck in 40 BC, and a further examination in Martini (1988b) 33ff.

    510. 950.56.1 9 21.20 g. From the same dies as Adolph Hess (1932) taf. 1.143. Martini (1988a) tav. XIV.tipo I; Martini (1988b) 98, mint of Lugdunum.

    511. 912x17.18 10 8.95 g. Imitation. Martini (1988) tav. XV.tipo IV; Martini (1988b) 104, struck in central Italy?

    512. 912x17.2 10.5 7.09 g. Imitation. Martini (1988) tav. XV.tipo IV; as above.

IMP.CAESAR DIVI F IIIVIR ITER.R.P.C.COS.ITER.ET TERT.DESIG   Mint: moving with Octavian. 37 BC

    Denarius. Obv.: head of Octavian r.; around ◯, IMP·CAESAR·DIVI·F·III·VIR·ITER·R·P ·C . Rev.: *simpulum, aspergillum*, jug, and *lituus*; above, COS·ITER·ET·TER· DESIG . Crawford 538/1.

    513. 950.56.226 1.5 3.65 g.

M.ANT.IMP.TERT.COS.DESIG.ITER.ET.TERT III VIR R.P.C   Mints: north coast of Syria and Greece (see Amandry [1990] 72–9, where Athens is suggested as the mint for Oppius Capito)

    As. Obv.: jugate heads of M. Antonius and Octavia r.; around, M·ANT·IM·ERT·COS·DESIG·ER·ET·ER·III·VIR R·P ·C or var. Rev.: ship r.; below, A and gorgon's head; around, M·OP P IVS·CAP ITO P ROP R·P RAEF·CLASS·F·C· or var. Bahrfeldt (1905) 22.21; *BMCRR* II 519.165-71; Sydenham 1268. For bibliography and discussion, see Crawford (1985) 254 and Amandry (1986), (1987), and (1990).

    514. 969x134.178 12 4.64 g.
    Publ.: Amandry (1987) 108.24 with obv. D12 and rev. K15 in the light series possibly dating to after Capito's return from Sicily at the end of 36/35 BC, see Amandry (1990) 83.

    515. 969x134.179 1 3.68 g.
    Publ.: Amandry (1987) 109.62 with obv. D27, die linked to 6 other specimens, and rev. R36, die linked to 7 other specimens. Light series as No. 514.

ANT.AVG.IIIVIR R.P.C   Mint: moving with M. Antonius. 32–31 BC

    Denarius. Obv.: ship r.; above, ANT·AVG ; below, III·VIR·R·P ·C . Rev.: *aquila* between two standards; below, legionary designation.

    516. 969x134.159 6 3.39 g (s.g. 9.157). Obv.: punchmark. Rev.: LEG III . Crawford 544/15.

    517. 950.56.280 10.5 3.35 g (s.g. 9.369). Rev.: LEG VI . Crawford 544/19. Ex O'Hagan Collection, Sotheby (1908) lot 977.

    518. 969x134.161 6.5 3.68 g (s.g. 10.012). Obv.: punchmarks. Rev.: LEG VII . Crawford 544/20.

    519. 969x134.165 8 3.30 g (s.g. 9.318). Rev.: as No. 518.

    520. 969x134.160 6.5 3.57 g (s.g. 9.909). Rev.: LEG X . Crawford 544/24.

    521. 969x134.162 7 2.77 g (s.g. 9.698). Part of flan clipped. Obv.: punchmark. Rev.: LEG XII(?) . Crawford 544/26.

    522. 969x134.164 11.5 3.20 g (s.g. 9.187). Rev.: LEG XV . Crawford 544/30.

    523. 969x134.163 6 3.32 g (s.g. 9.086). Rev.: LEG XVI . Crawford 544/31.

    524. 950.56.227 6.5 3.47 g (s.g. 10.181). Obv.: punchmark. Rev.: LEG XX ; punchmark. Crawford 544/36. Ex O'Hagan Collection, Sotheby (1908) lot 977.

APPENDICES

APPENDIX A:
AES RUDE

Aes Rude. Irregularly shaped pieces of bronze of unknown date, see Haeberlin (1910) taf.1-4.8 and Thomsen (1961) 200–202 and fig. 48.
> A1. 921.62.60 46.27 g. Length, 32.3 mm; width, 26.4 mm; height, 9.9 mm.
> A2. 921.62.61 23.68 g. Length, 23 mm; width, 20.7 mm; height, 10.7 mm. Ex Weber Collection, Forrer (1922) no. 112.

APPENDIX B:
ITALIC CAST BRONZE COINS

VOLATERRAE, ETRURIA
Quadrans. Obv.: young janiform head wearing petasus. Rev.: club between ·· ; around, I◄OA↓∃∃ . From the period of the First Punic War (264–241 BC), see Crawford (1985) 46. Haeberlin (1910) taf. 84.6–7; Sydenham (1926) 127.309; Thurlow and Vecchi (1979) 38.89.
> B1. 912x17.24 6 31 g.

UNCERTAIN OF ETRURIA
Quadrans. Obv.: wheel with five spokes; in one interstice, Ɔ . Rev.: anchor; in field, ··· . From the period of the First Punic War, see No. B1. Haeberlin (1910) taf. 89.9–10; Sydenham (1926) 125.280; Thurlow and Vecchi (1979) 38.118.
> B2. 969x134.188 12 33.59 g.

TUDER, UMBRIA
Semis. Obv.: sleeping dog; on l., ∃◄†V† . Rev.: lyre; in l. field, Ɔ . From the period of the Second Punic War (218–201 BC). Haeberlin (1910) taf. 81.10–13; Sydenham (1926) 118.219; Thurlow and Vecchi (1979) 39.164.
> B3. 912x17.19 1 37.40 g.

PERHAPS VOLSINII
Sextans. Obv.: club. Rev.: two dots. Haeberlin (1910) taf. 81.36–41; Sydenham (1926) 120.243; SNG Copenhagen (1942), pl. 2.78–80, after 268 BC; Thurlow and Vecchi (1979) 39.172, 225–213 BC; perhaps Volsinii, period of the First Punic War, M. Crawford, pers. comm., 1991.
> B4. 969x134.46 21.70 g.

LUCERIA, APULIA
Quincunx. Obv.: equal-armed cross. Rev.: as obv. but with five dots in one interstice and L in the opposite interstice. From the period of the Second Punic War, see Crawford (1985) 45. Haeberlin (1910) taf. 71.14–17; Sydenham (1926) 108.138; Thurlow and Vecchi (1979) 41.281.
> B5. 969x134.185 36.89 g.

APPENDIX C:
ITALIC ISSUES OF THE SOCIAL WAR, 91–87 BC

Denarius. Obv.: helmeted head of Italia r.; below chin, X . Rev.: Dioscuri on horseback r.; in exergue, VII∃T∃ . According to Crawford (1964) 145–46, this issue was the earliest of the series and would therefore date to 91 BC but it has since been placed at Corfinium in 90 BC, see Campana (1987) 50.
> C1. 950.56.149 3 3.90 g (s.g. 10.359). No. C1 is Campana (1987) 50.series 1.1d (D1, R1). Ex Naville IV lot 10.

Denarius. Obv.: laureate head of Italia l.; behind, VI◄∃T∃ downwards. Rev.: soldier standing, holding reversed spear and placing l. foot on Roman standard; on r., bull. According to Crawford (1964) 146, this issue is from 89 BC; Bovianum(?), 89 BC, see Campana (1987) 99.
> C2. 950.56.148   11 3.81 g (s.g. 10.420). Obv.: die flaw across face. Rev.: in exergue, I ; from same die as Lepczyk (1981) lot 629. From same dies as Lanz (1983) taf. 16.364 and Münzen und Medaillen (1989) 4.49. No. C2 is Campana (1987) 103.series 9b.136d (D93, R116). Ex Naville IV lot 9.
> C3. 950.56.232 4.5 3.77 g (s.g. 10.51). Obv.: from same die as *BMCRR* III pl. XCVIII.14. From same dies as Münzen und Medaillen (1986) 5.35. No. C3 is Campana (1987) 106.series 9b.147w (D99, R122).

PLATES

1

2

3

4

5

6

7

8

9

10   **11**

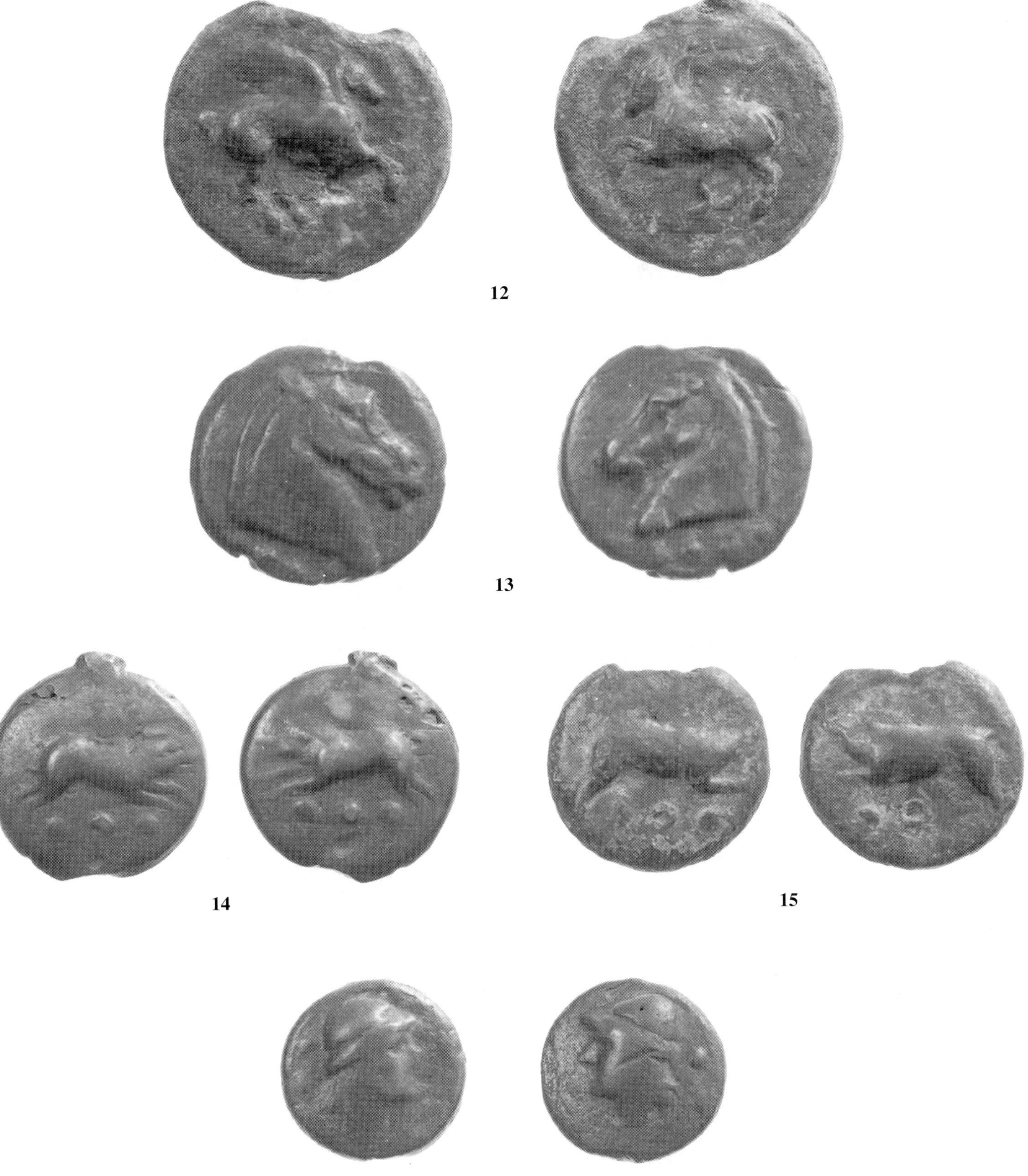

12

13

14

15

16

17

18

19

20

21

22

23

24

25

26

27

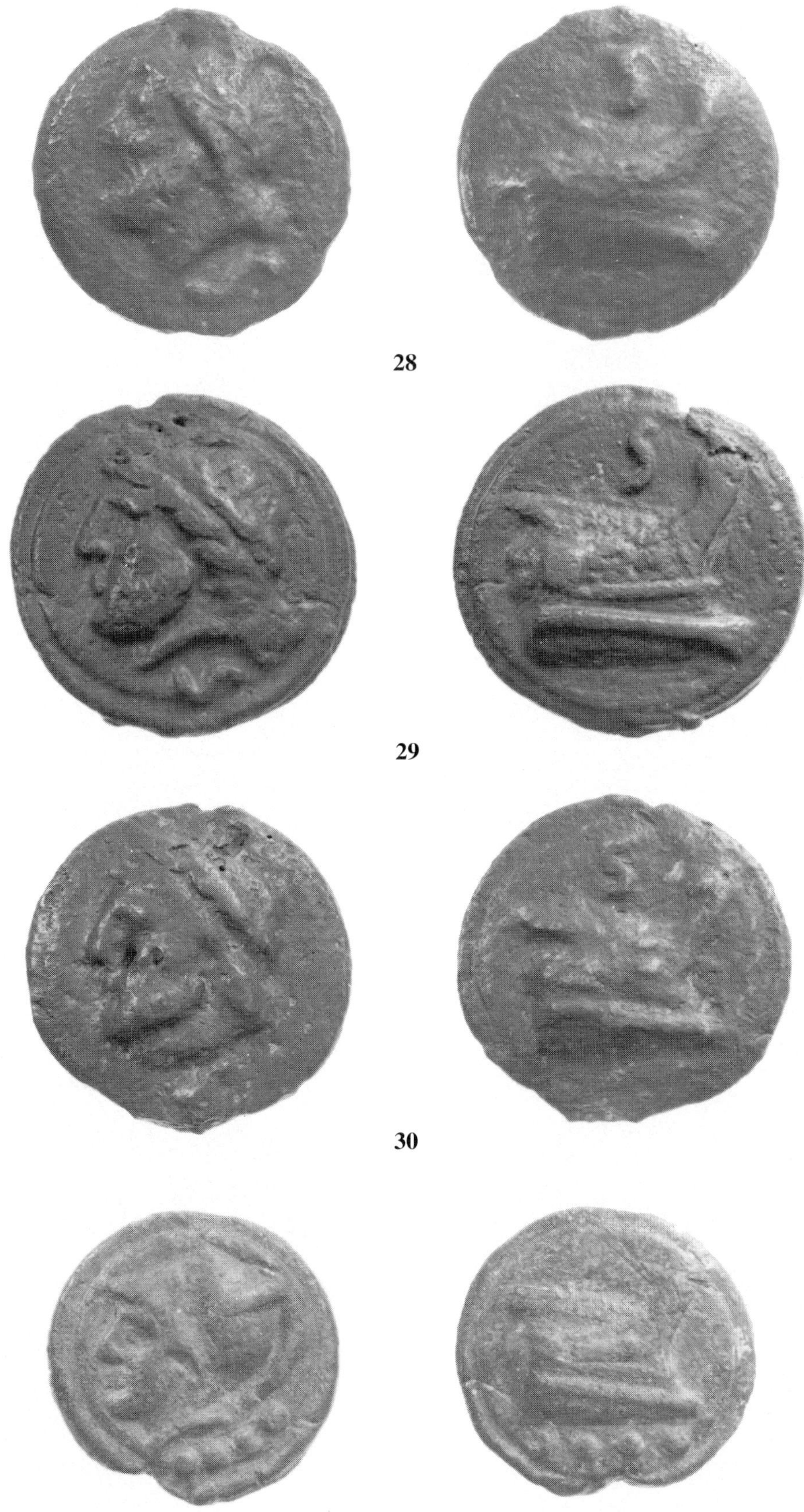

28

29

30

31

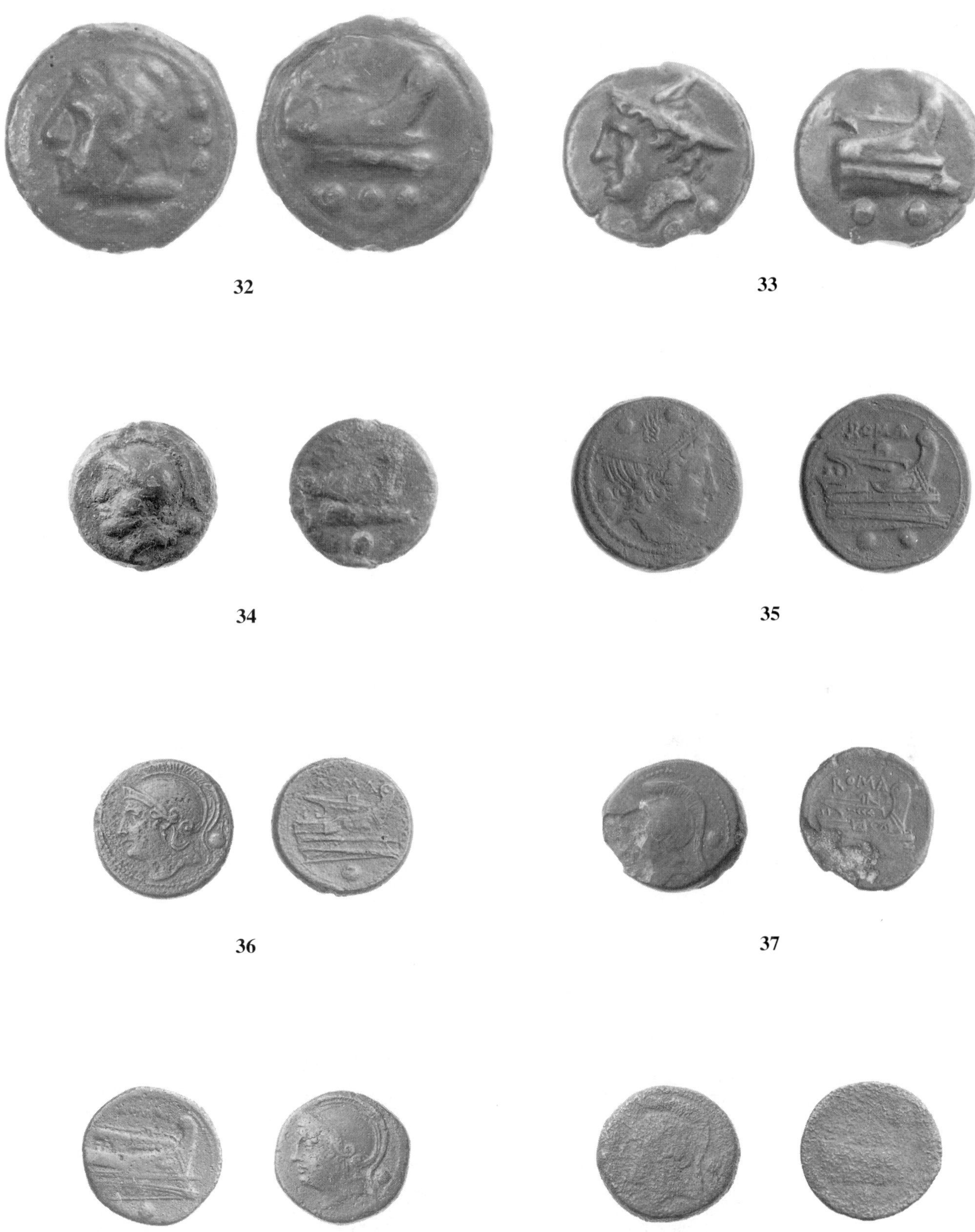

32

33

34

35

36

37

38

39

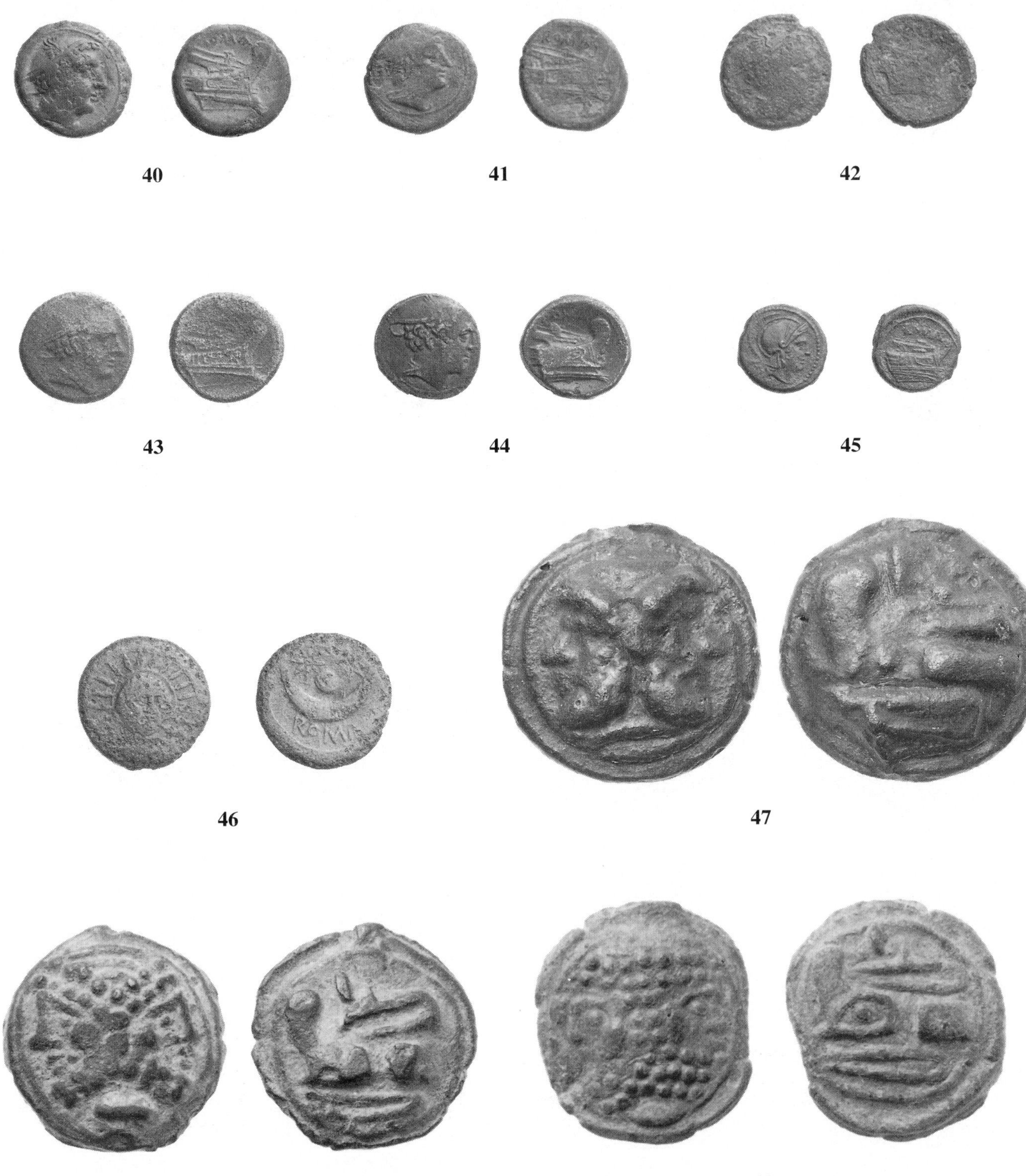

40

41

42

43

44

45

46

47

48

49

50

51

52

53

54

55

56

57

58

59

60

61

62

63

64

65

66

67

68

69

70

71

72

73

74

75

76

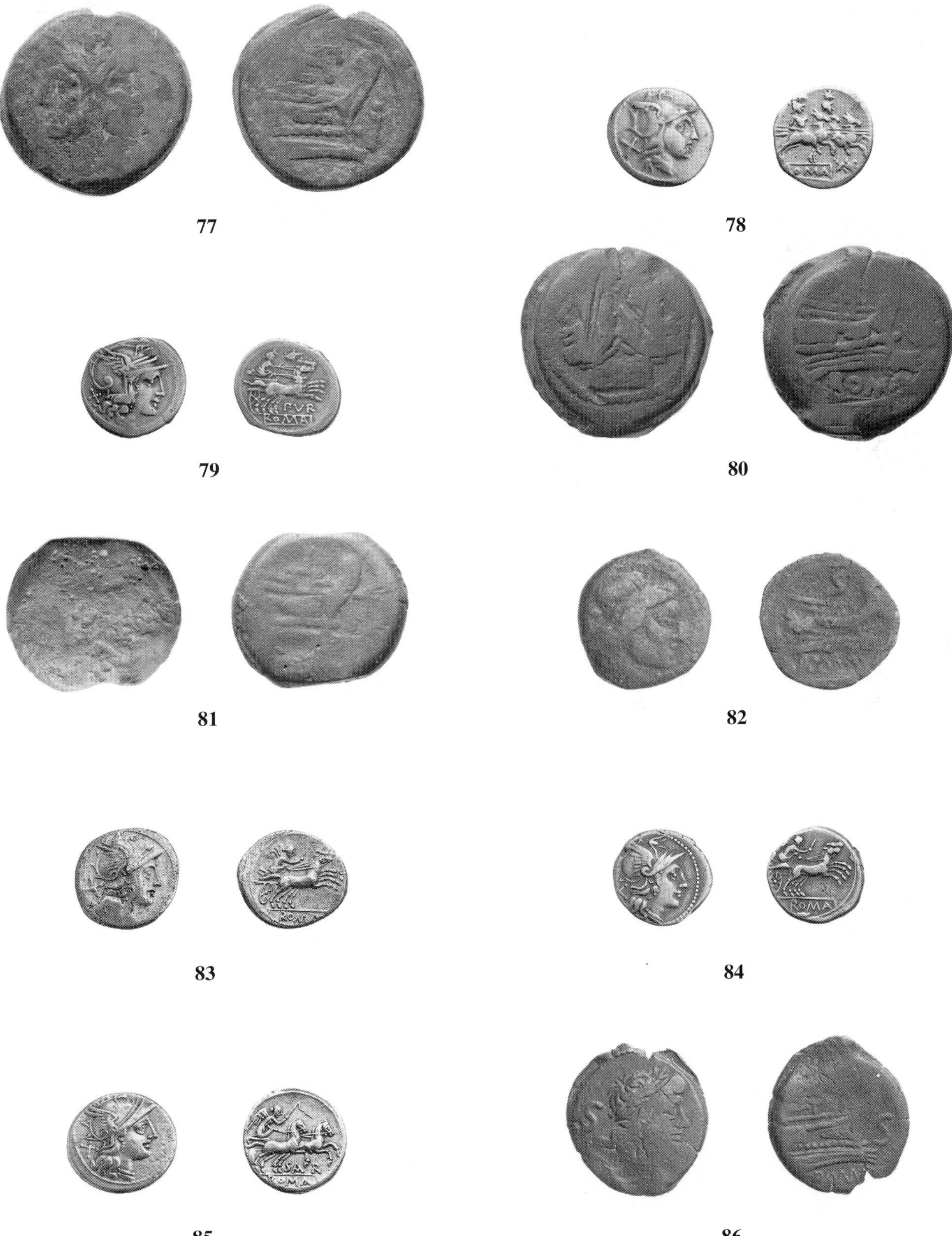

77

78

79

80

81

82

83

84

85

86

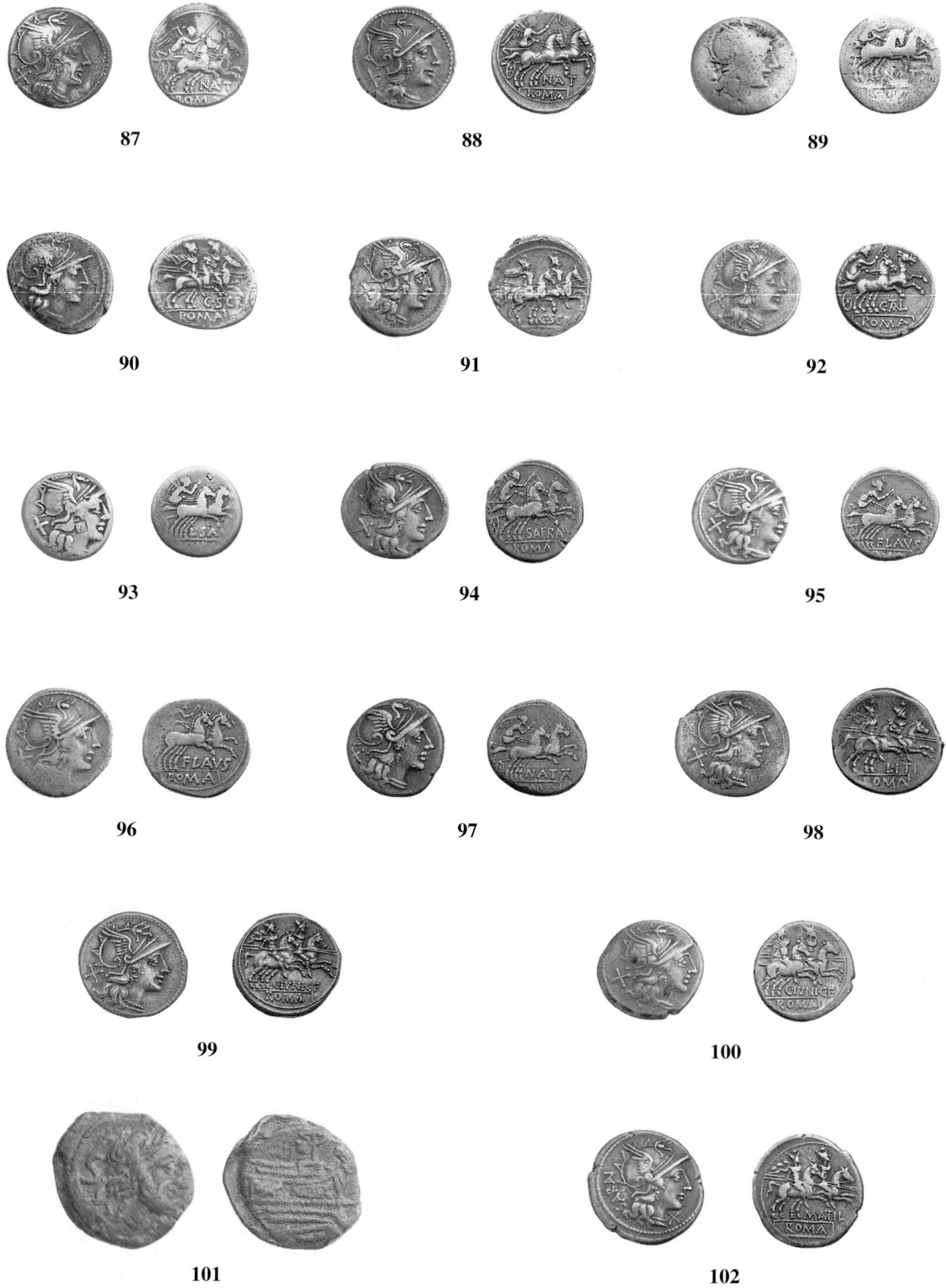

87

88

89

90

91

92

93

94

95

96

97

98

99

100

101

102

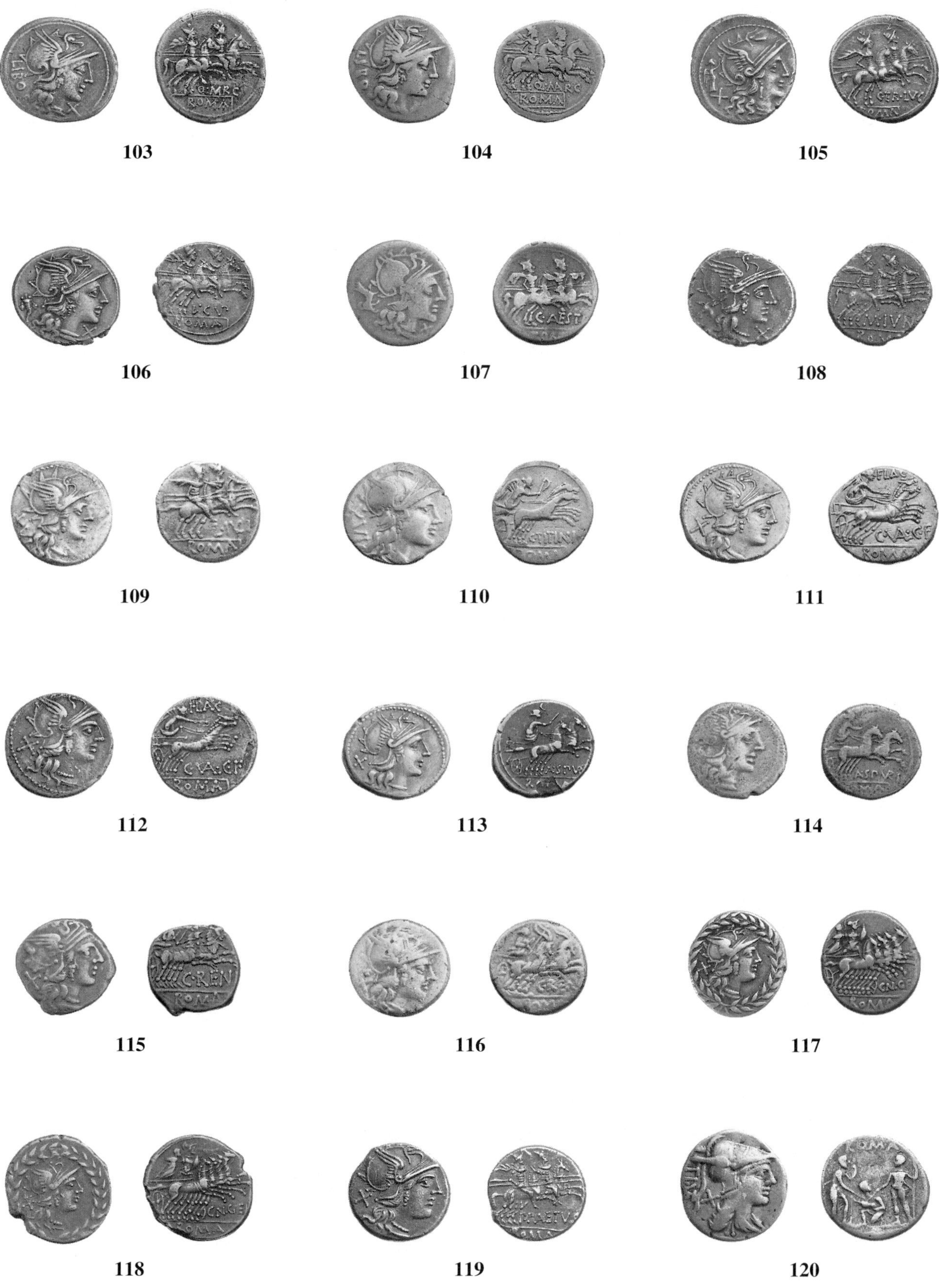

103

104

105

106

107

108

109

110

111

112

113

114

115

116

117

118

119

120

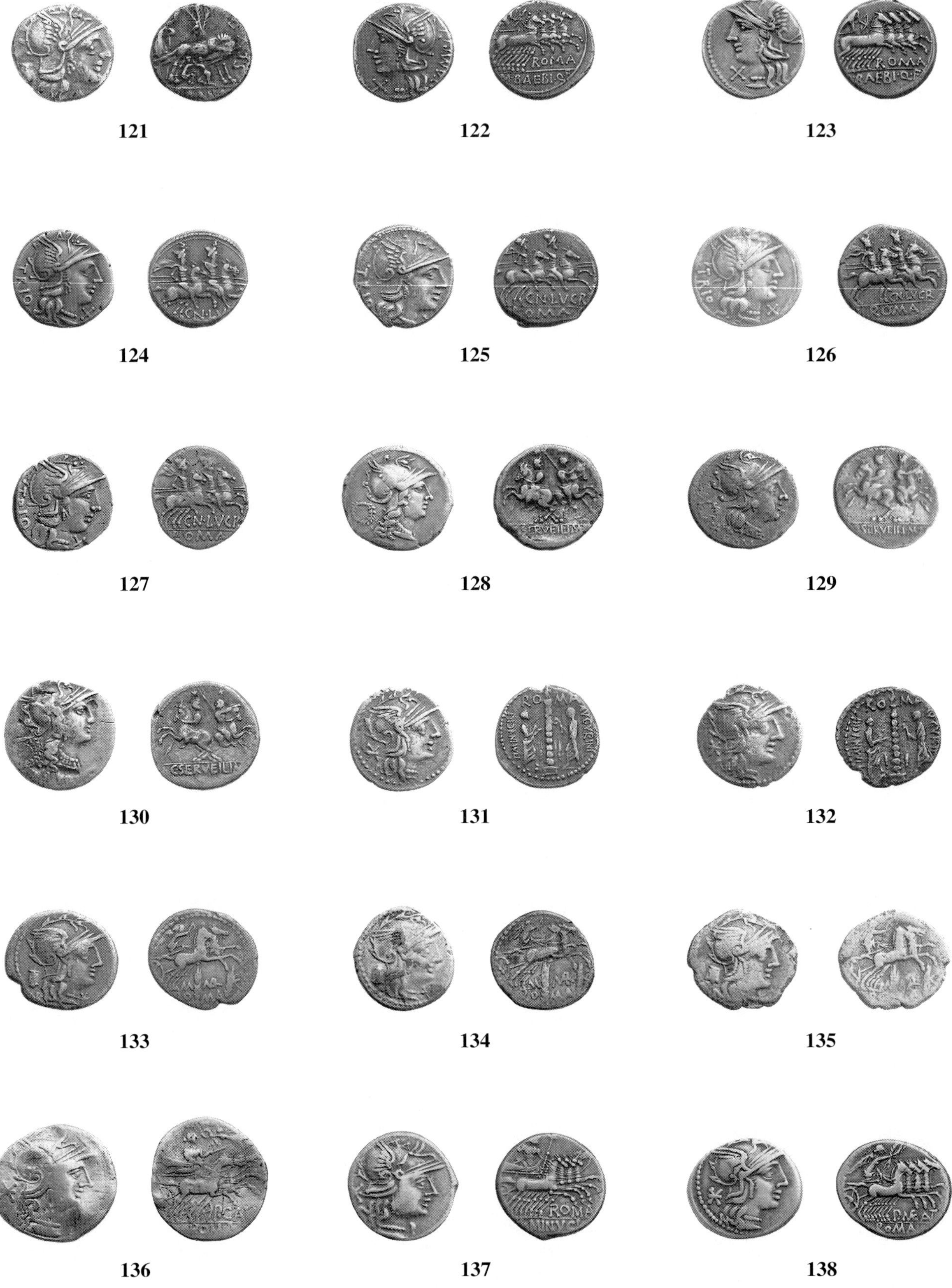

121

122

123

124

125

126

127

128

129

130

131

132

133

134

135

136

137

138

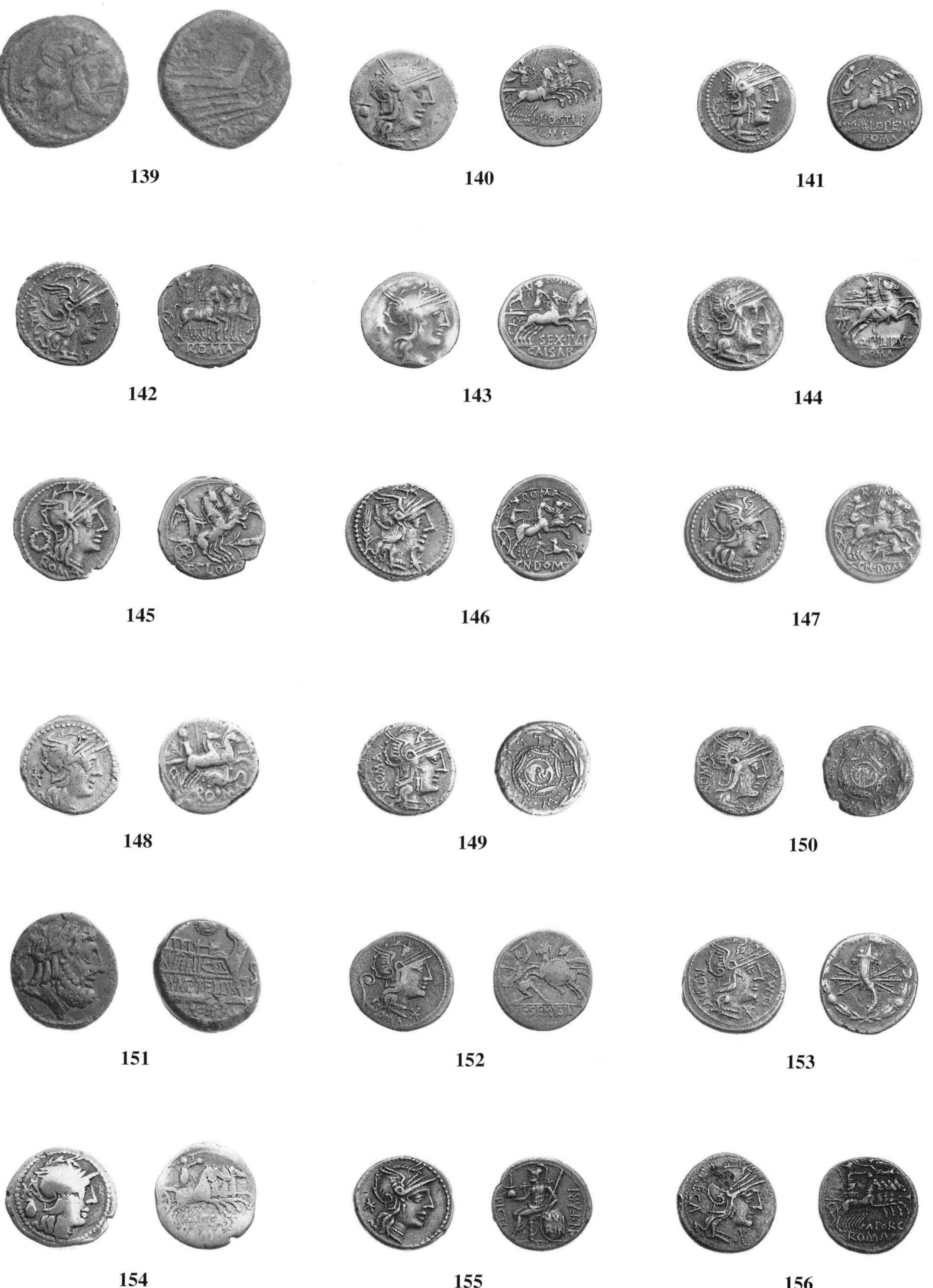

139

140

141

142

143

144

145

146

147

148

149

150

151

152

153

154

155

156

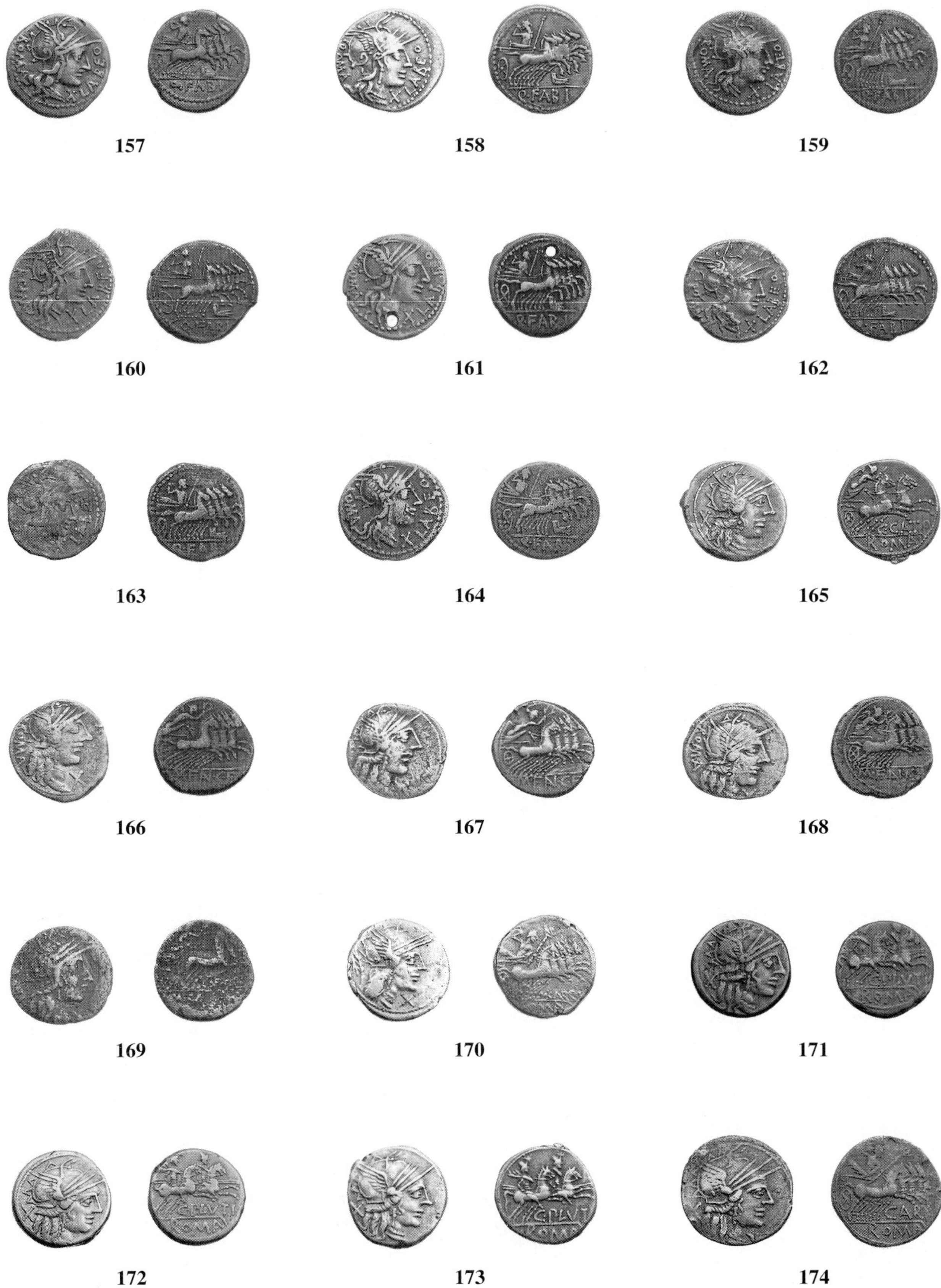

157 158 159

160 161 162

163 164 165

166 167 168

169 170 171

172 173 174

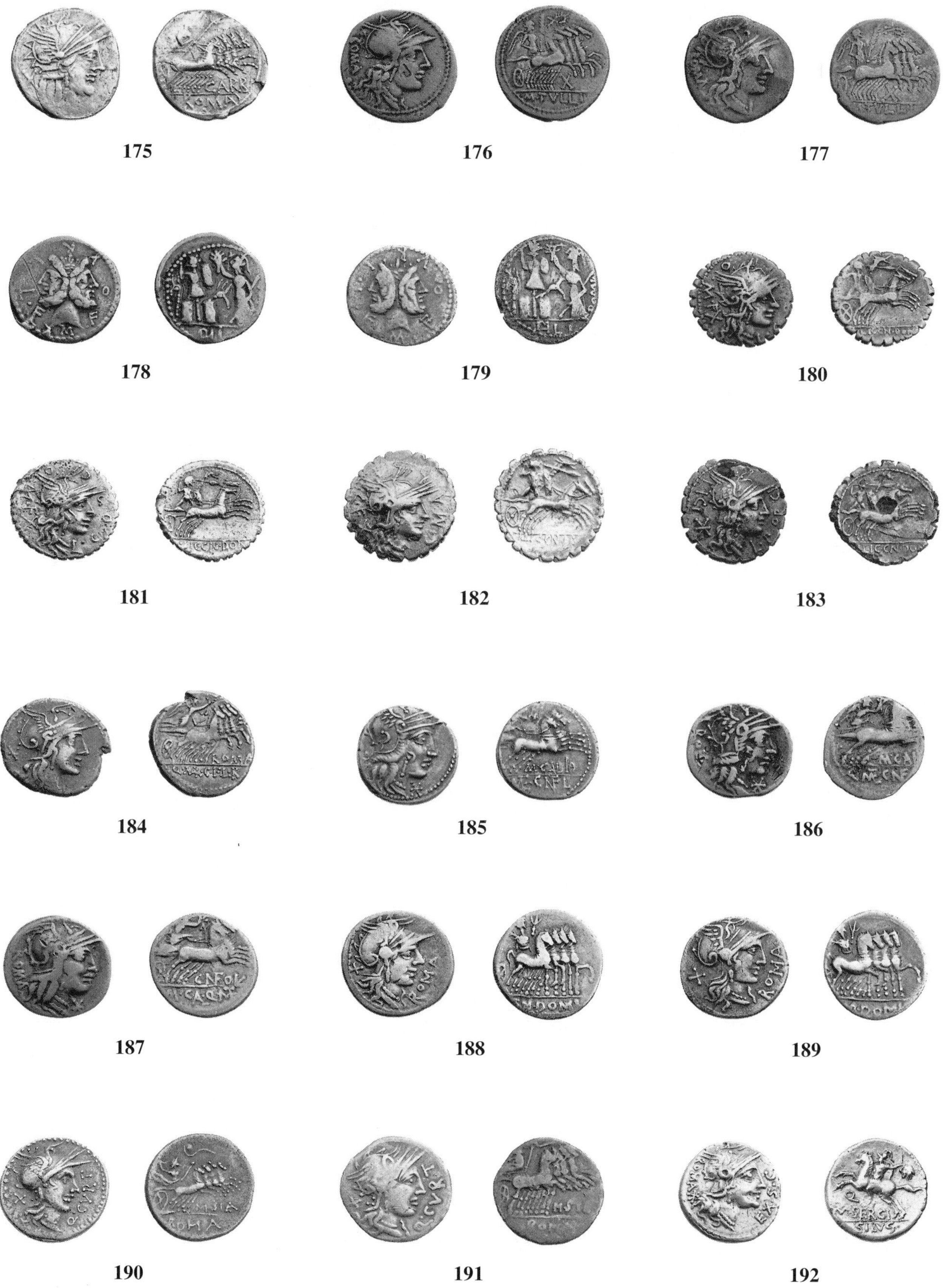

175

176

177

178

179

180

181

182

183

184

185

186

187

188

189

190

191

192

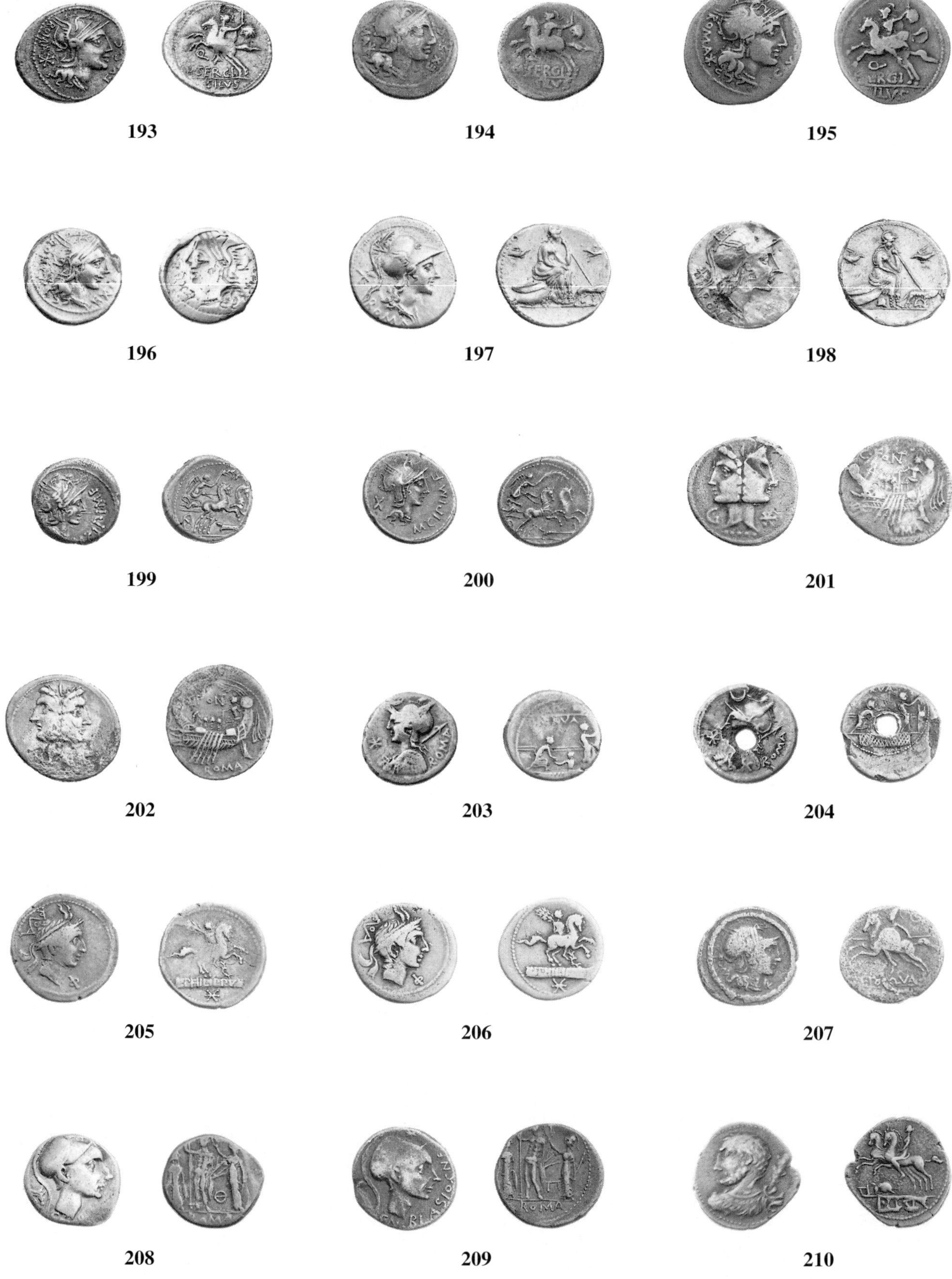

193

194

195

196

197

198

199

200

201

202

203

204

205

206

207

208

209

210

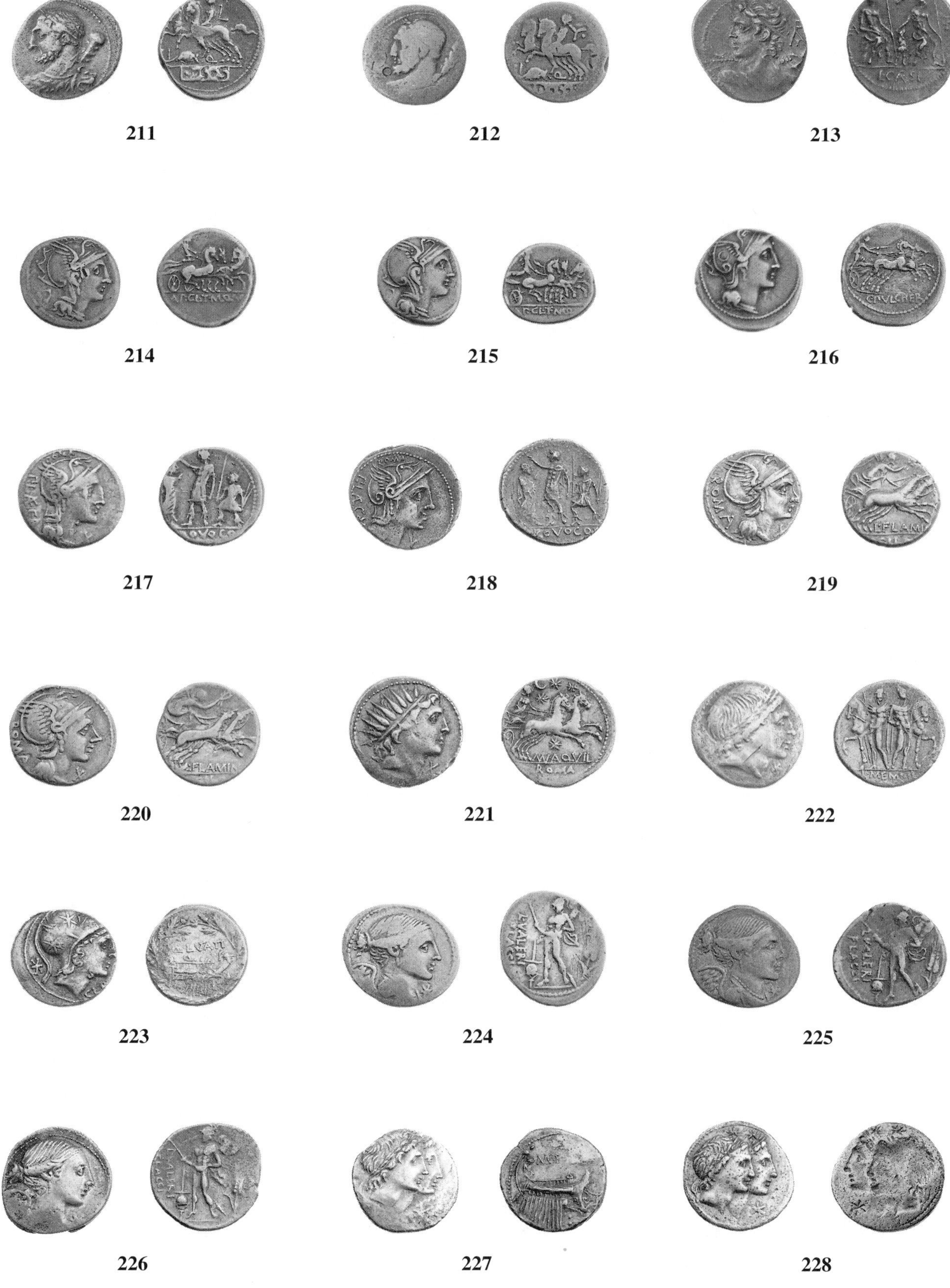

211

212

213

214

215

216

217

218

219

220

221

222

223

224

225

226

227

228

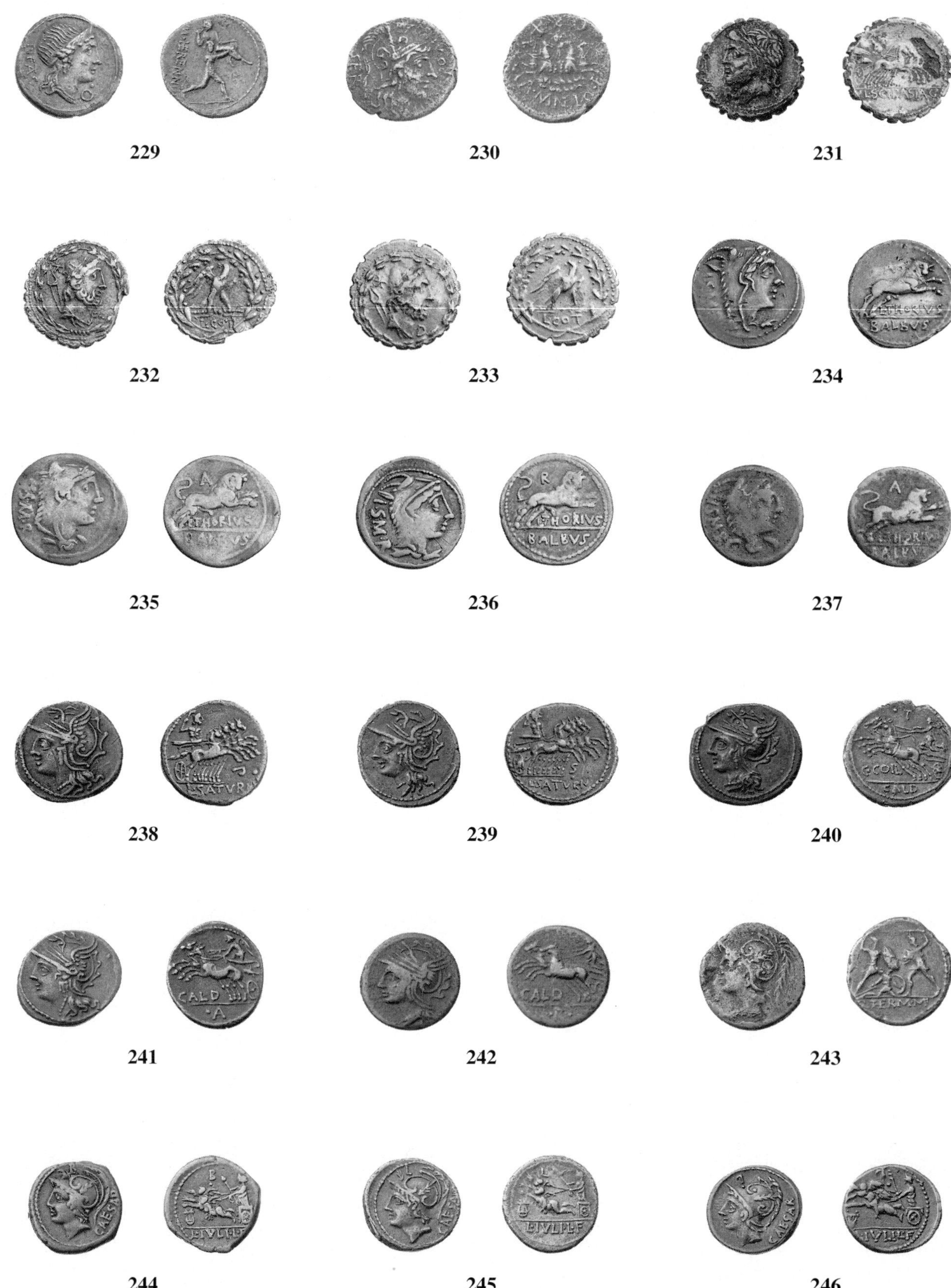

229

230

231

232

233

234

235

236

237

238

239

240

241

242

243

244

245

246

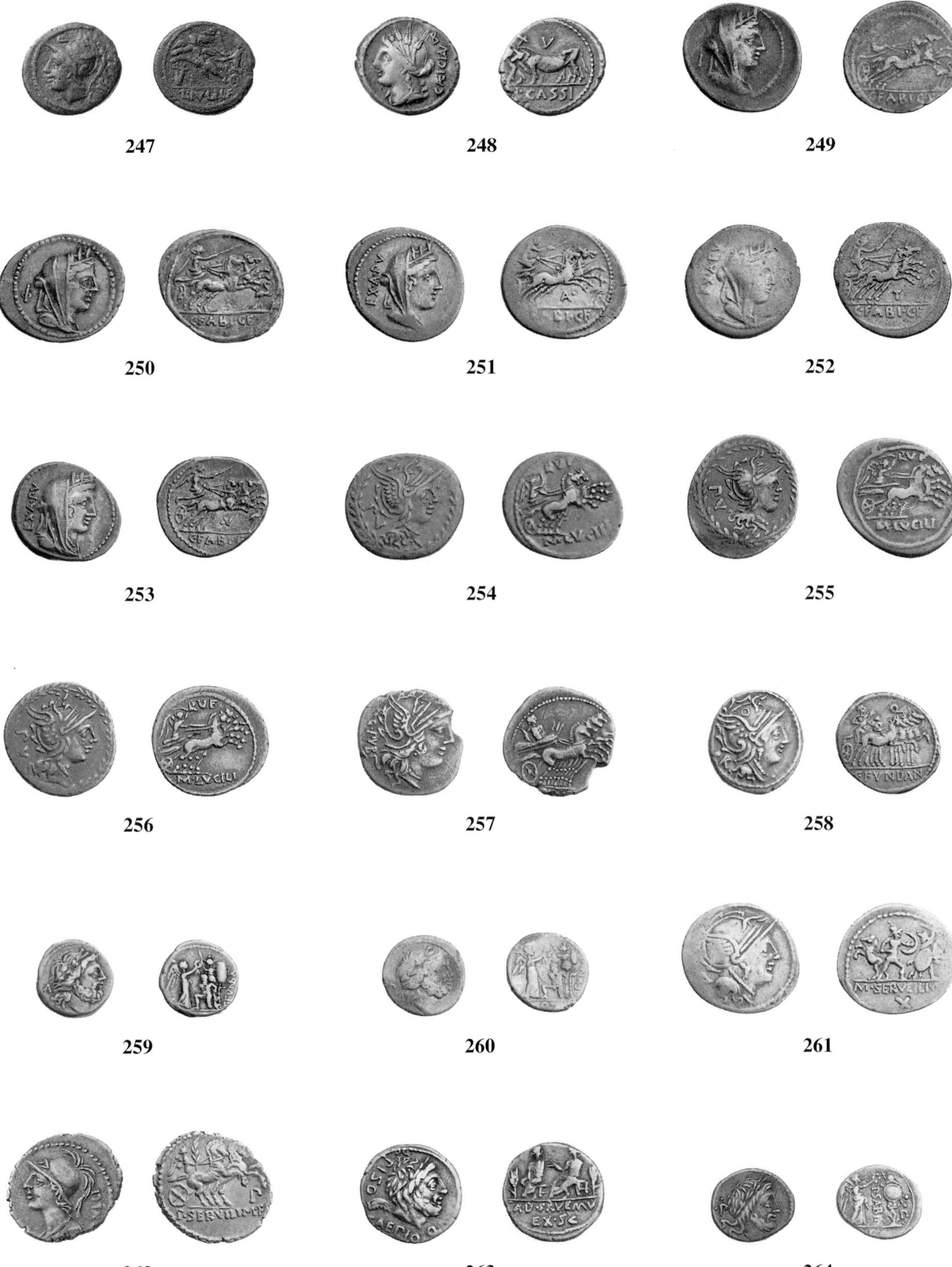

247

248

249

250

251

252

253

254

255

256

257

258

259

260

261

262

263

264

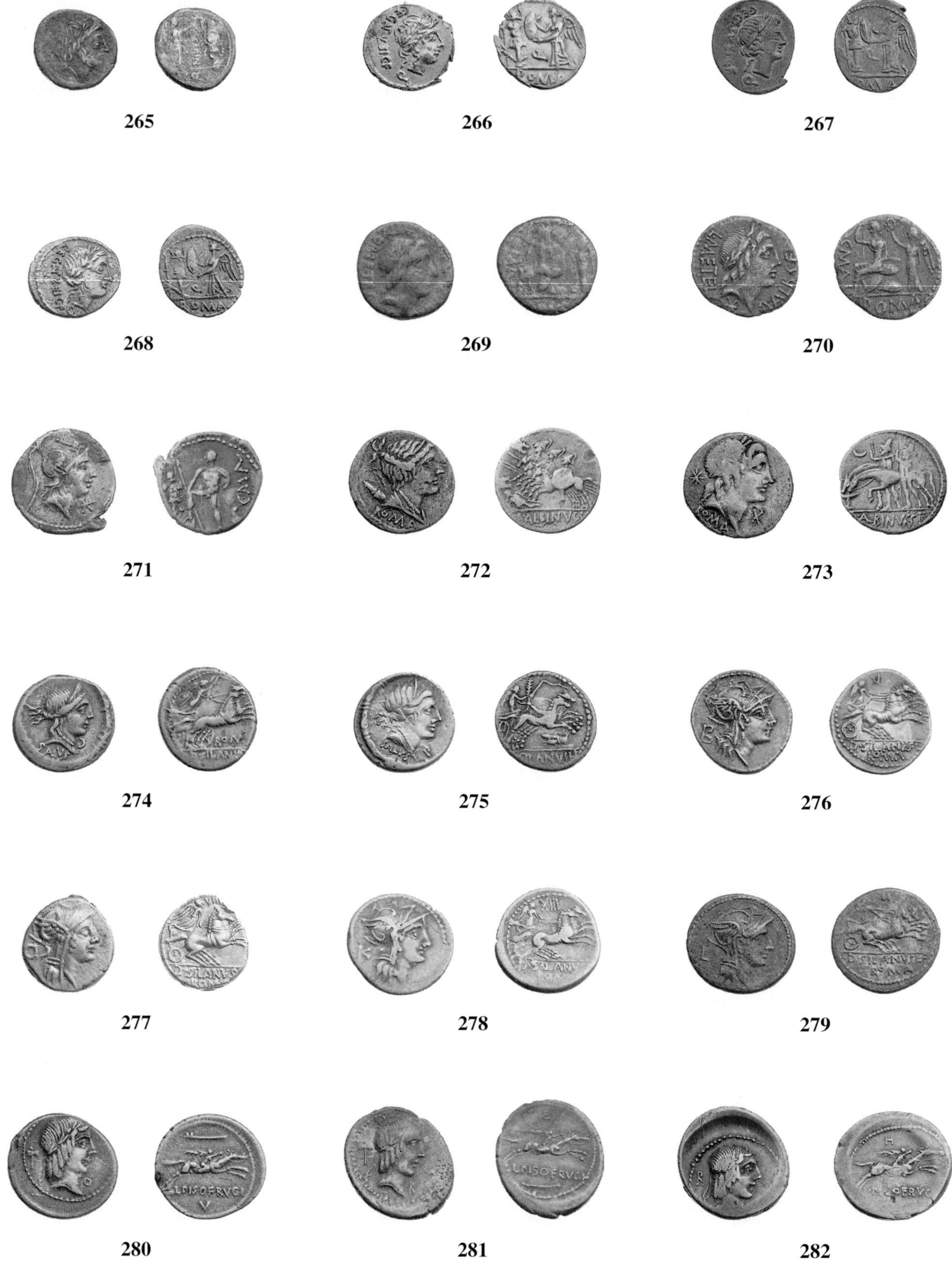

265

266

267

268

269

270

271

272

273

274

275

276

277

278

279

280

281

282

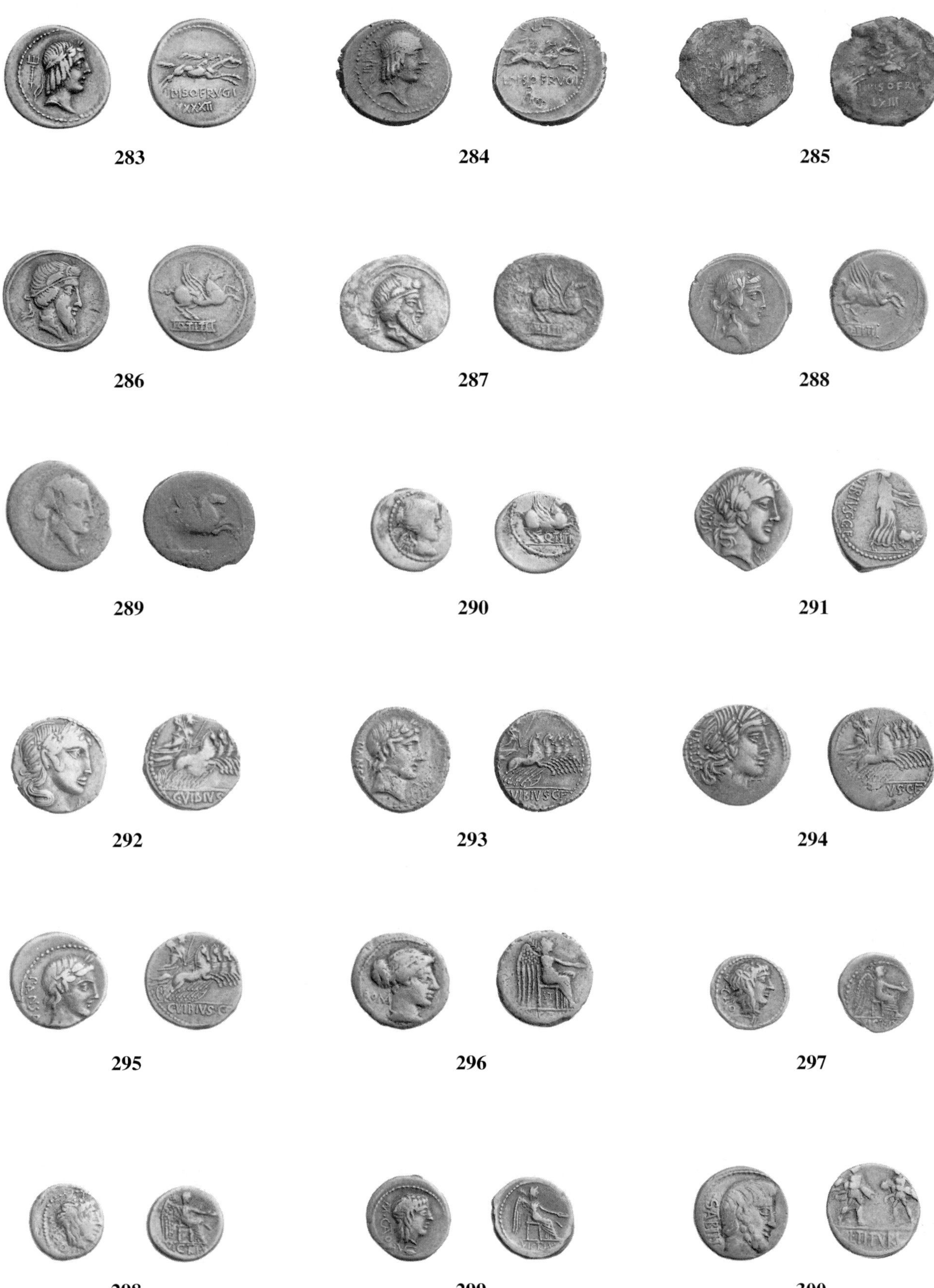

283

284

285

286

287

288

289

290

291

292

293

294

295

296

297

298

299

300

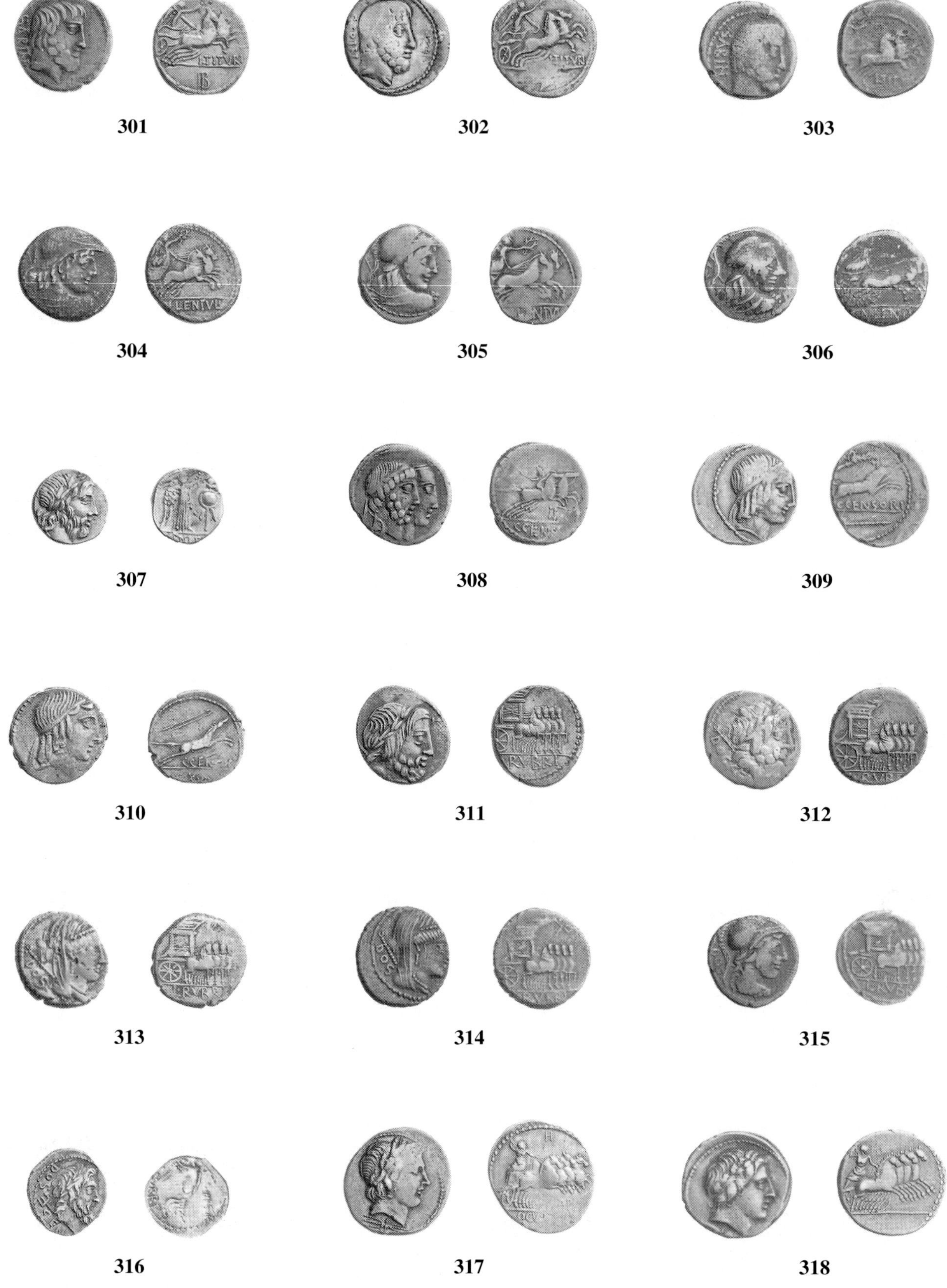

301

302

303

304

305

306

307

308

309

310

311

312

313

314

315

316

317

318

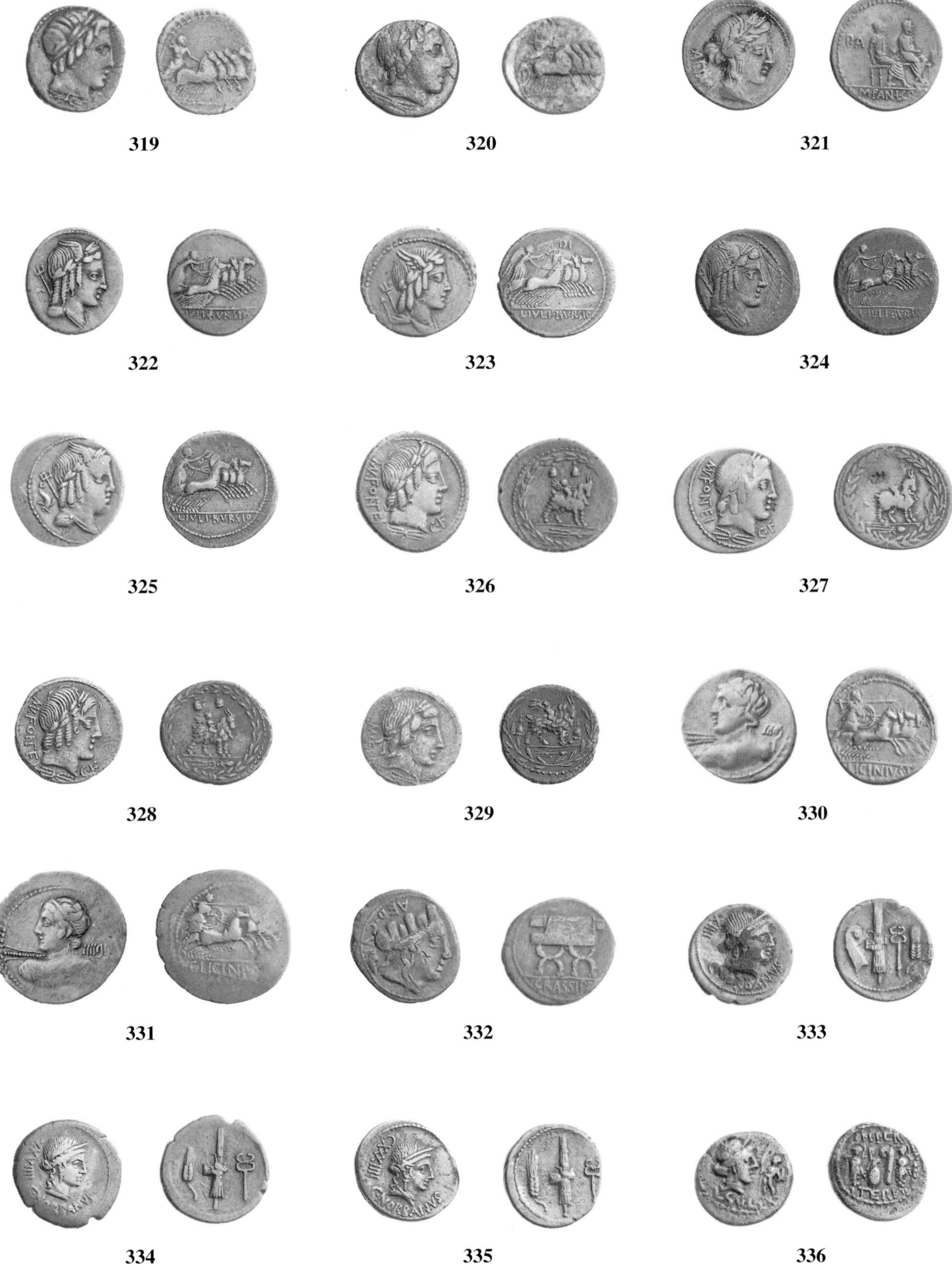

319   320   321

322   323   324

325   326   327

328   329   330

331   332   333

334   335   336

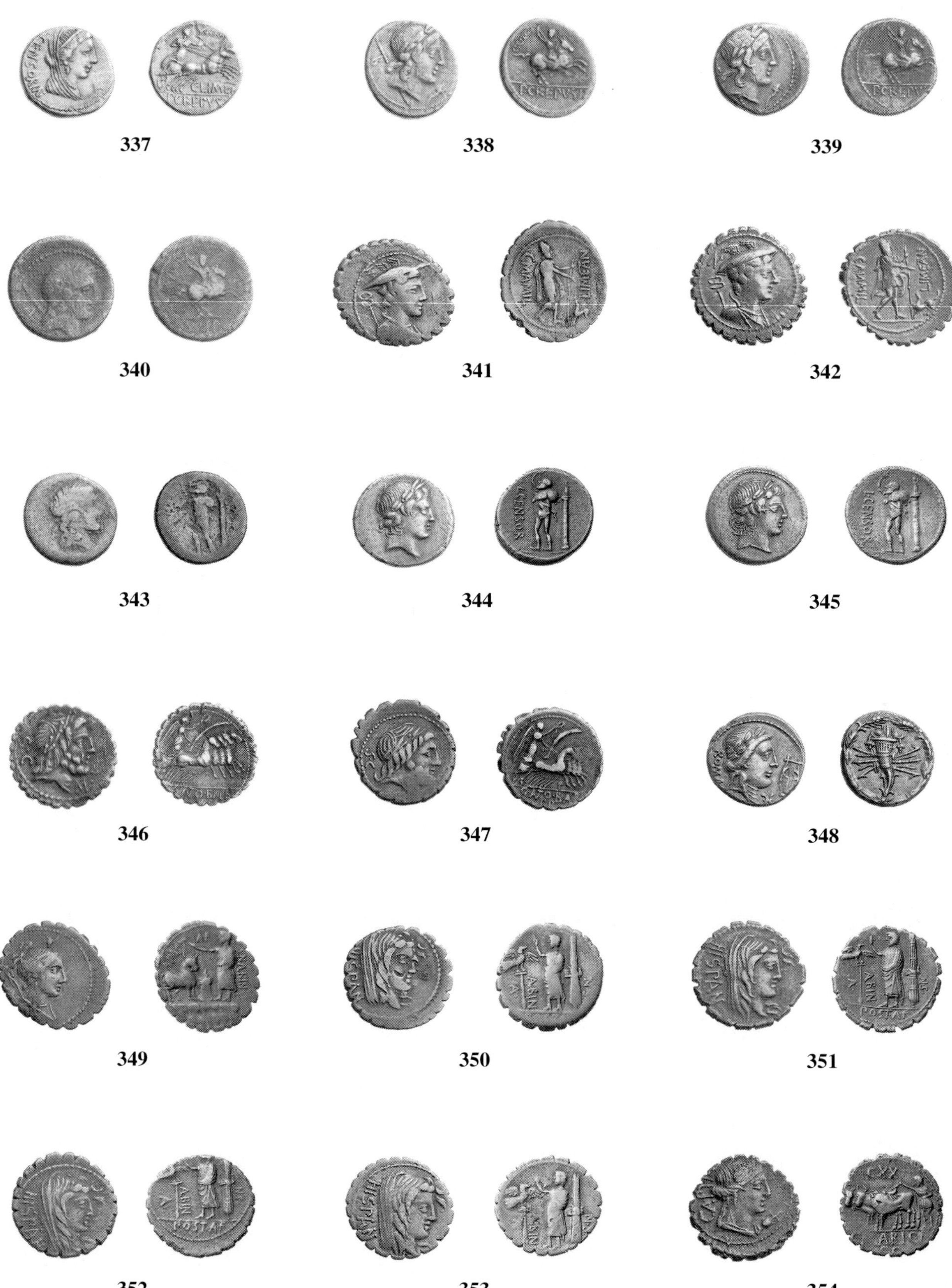

337

338

339

340

341

342

343

344

345

346

347

348

349

350

351

352

353

354

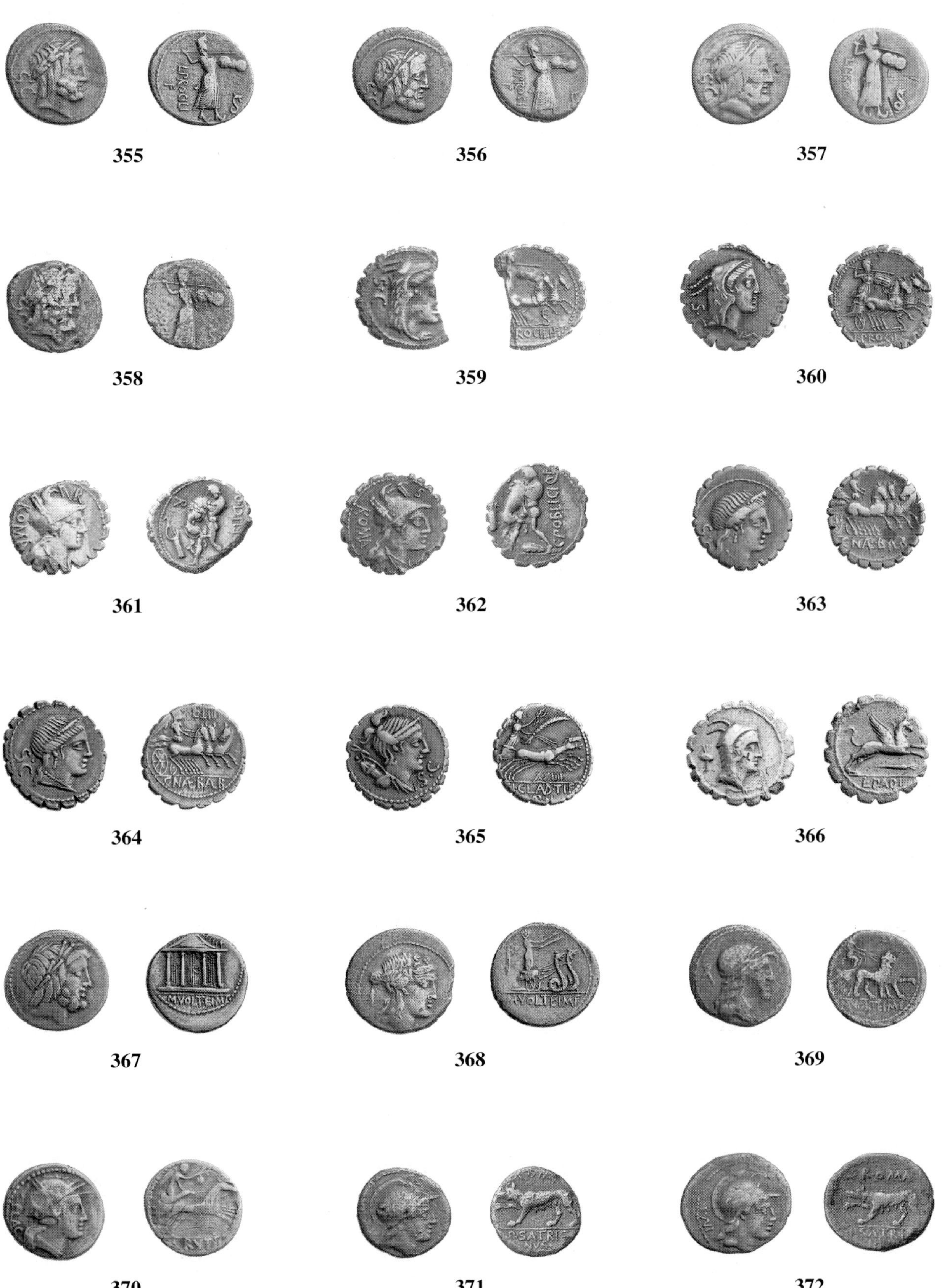

355

356

357

358

359

360

361

362

363

364

365

366

367

368

369

370

371

372

373

374

375

376

377

378

379

380

381

382

383

384

385

386

387

388

389

390

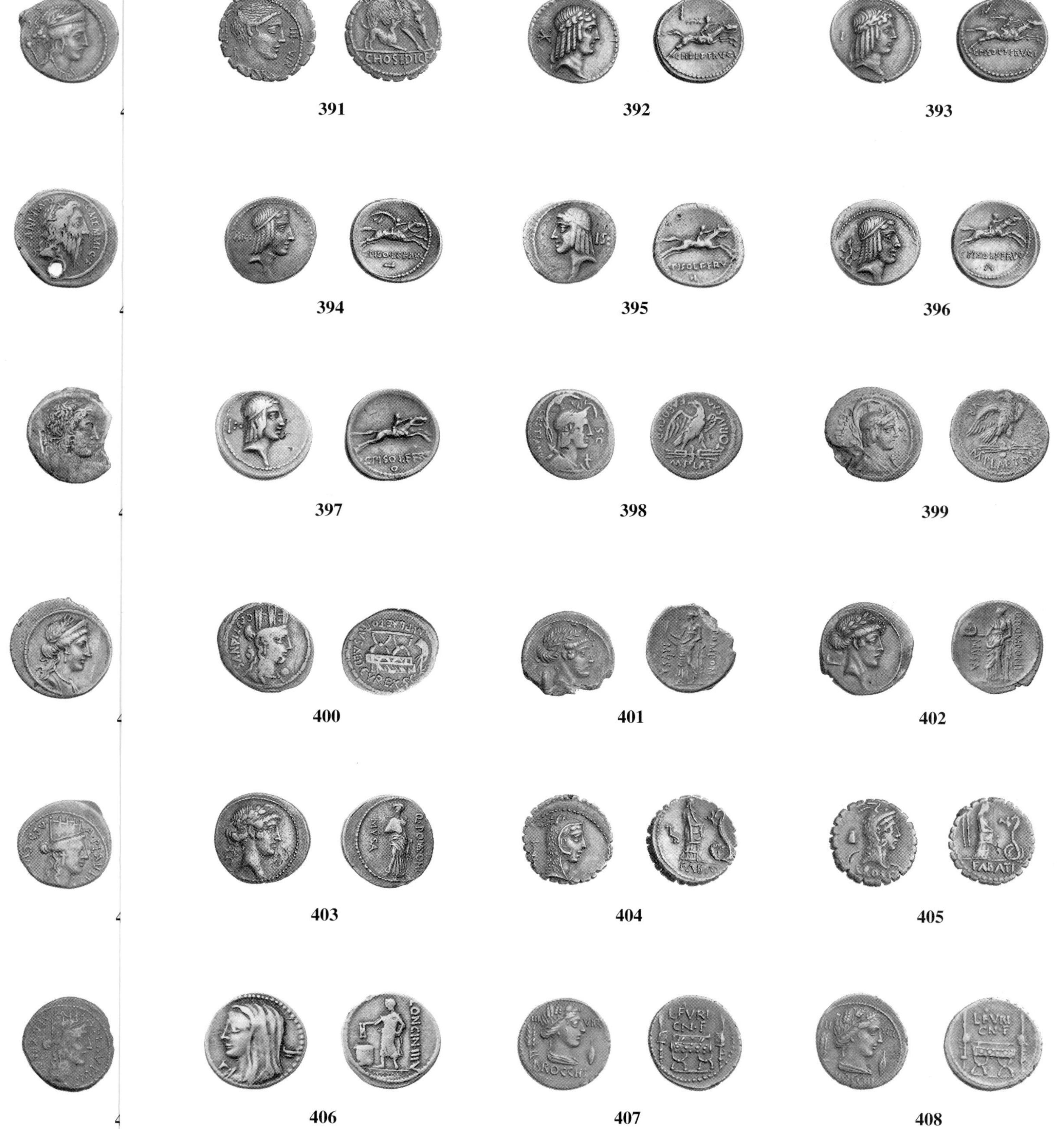

391

392

393

394

395

396

397

398

399

400

401

402

403

404

405

406

407

408

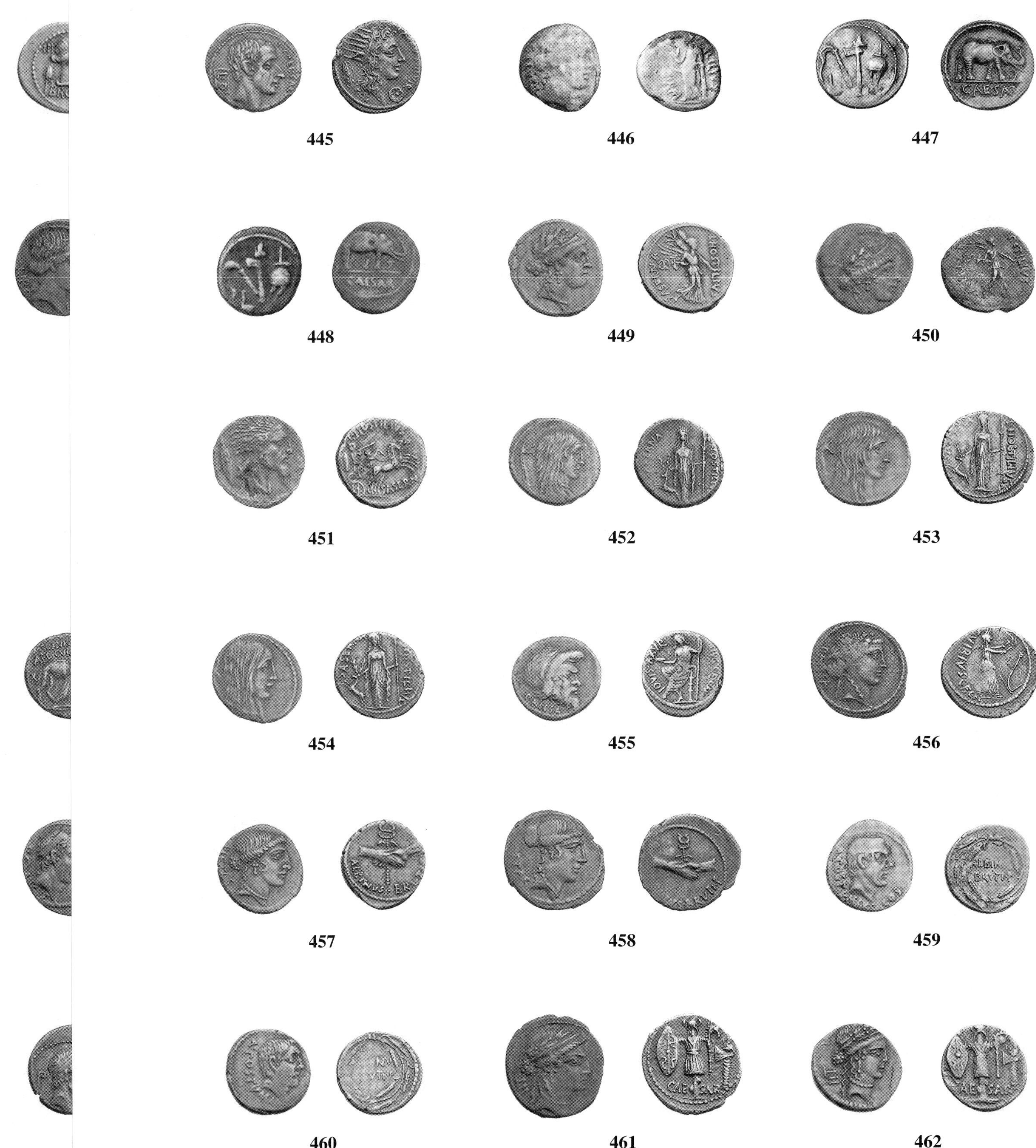

445

446

447

448

449

450

451

452

453

454

455

456

457

458

459

460

461

462

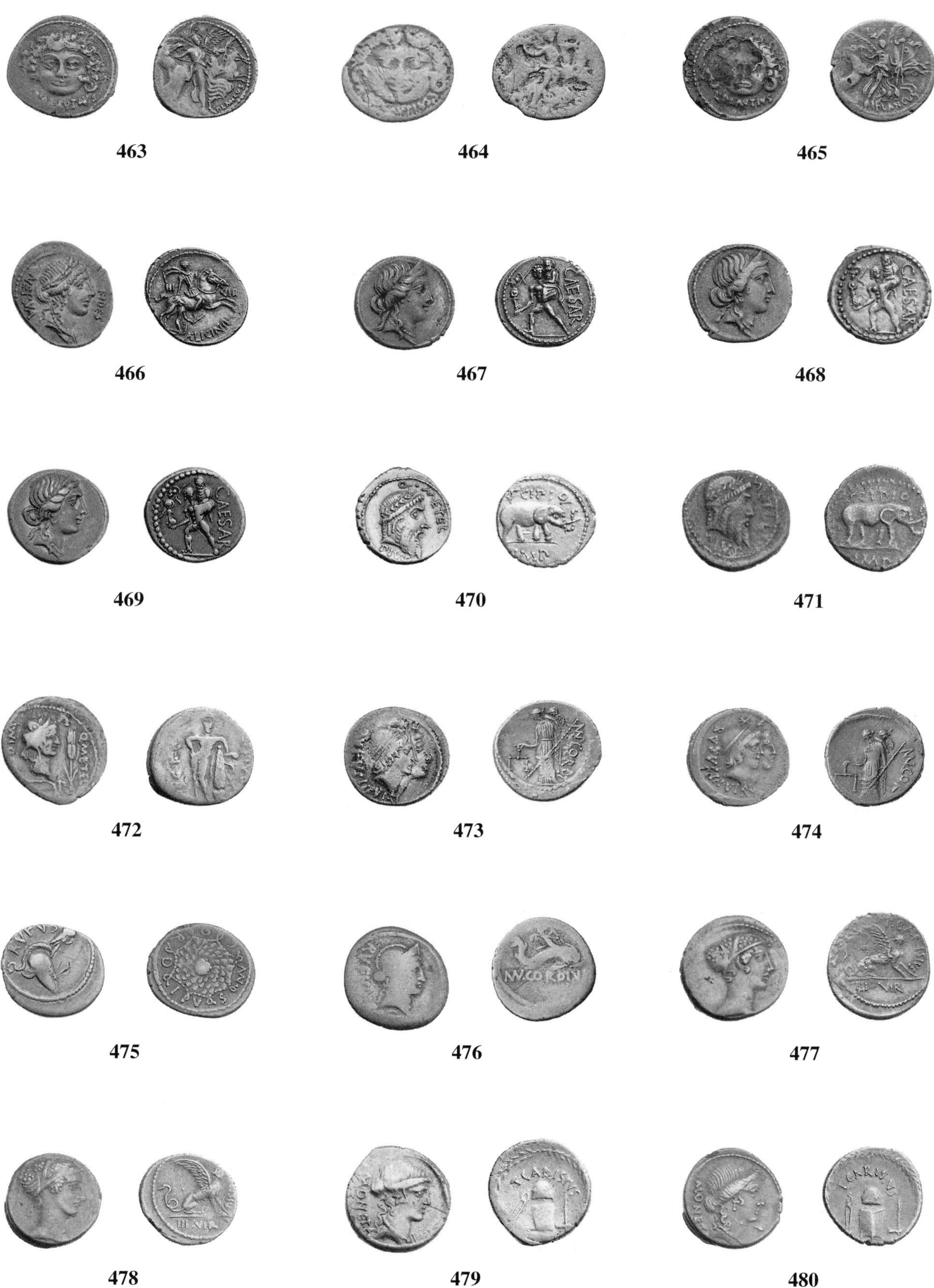

463

464

465

466

467

468

469

470

471

472

473

474

475

476

477

478

479

480

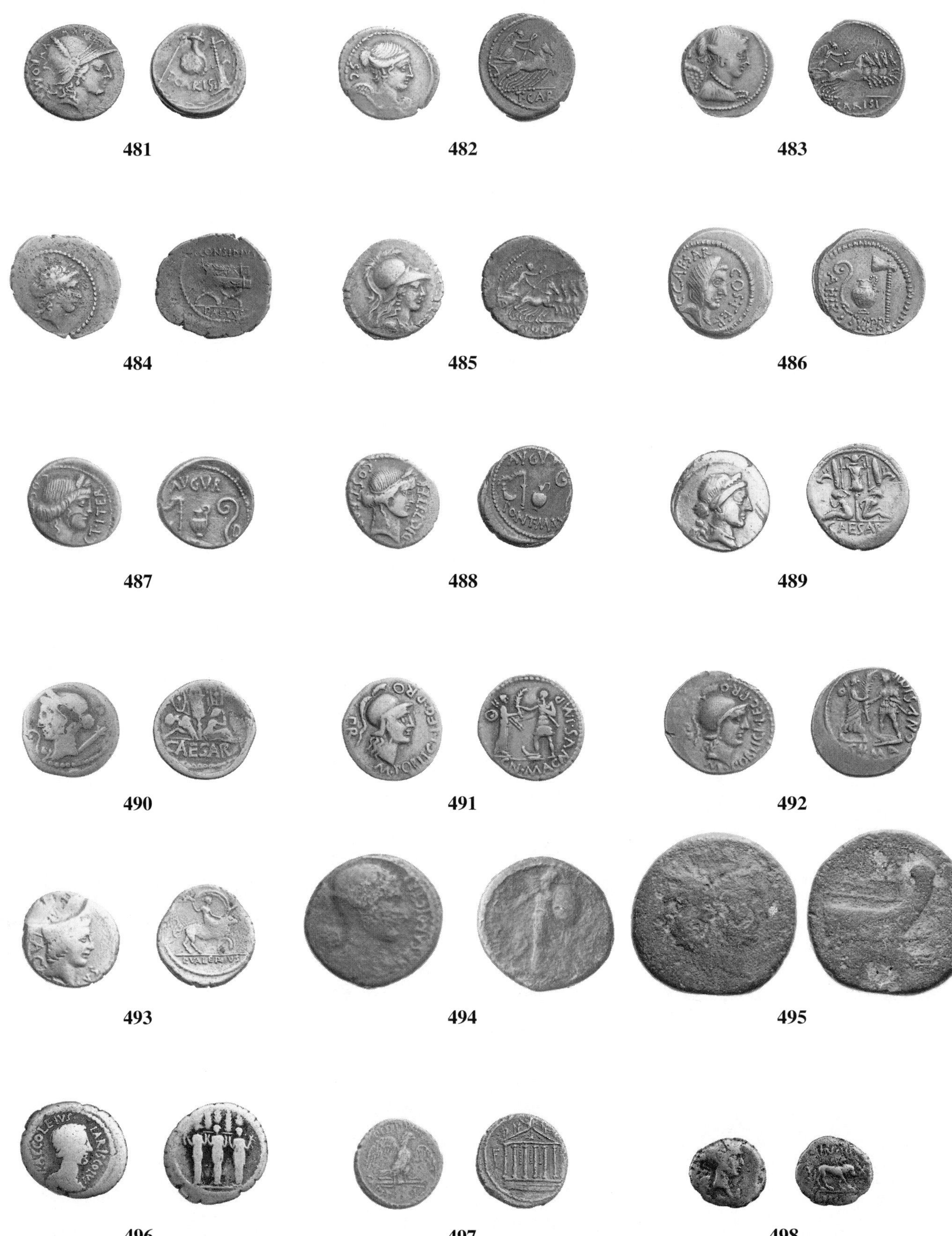

481

482

483

484

485

486

487

488

489

490

491

492

493

494

495

496

497

498

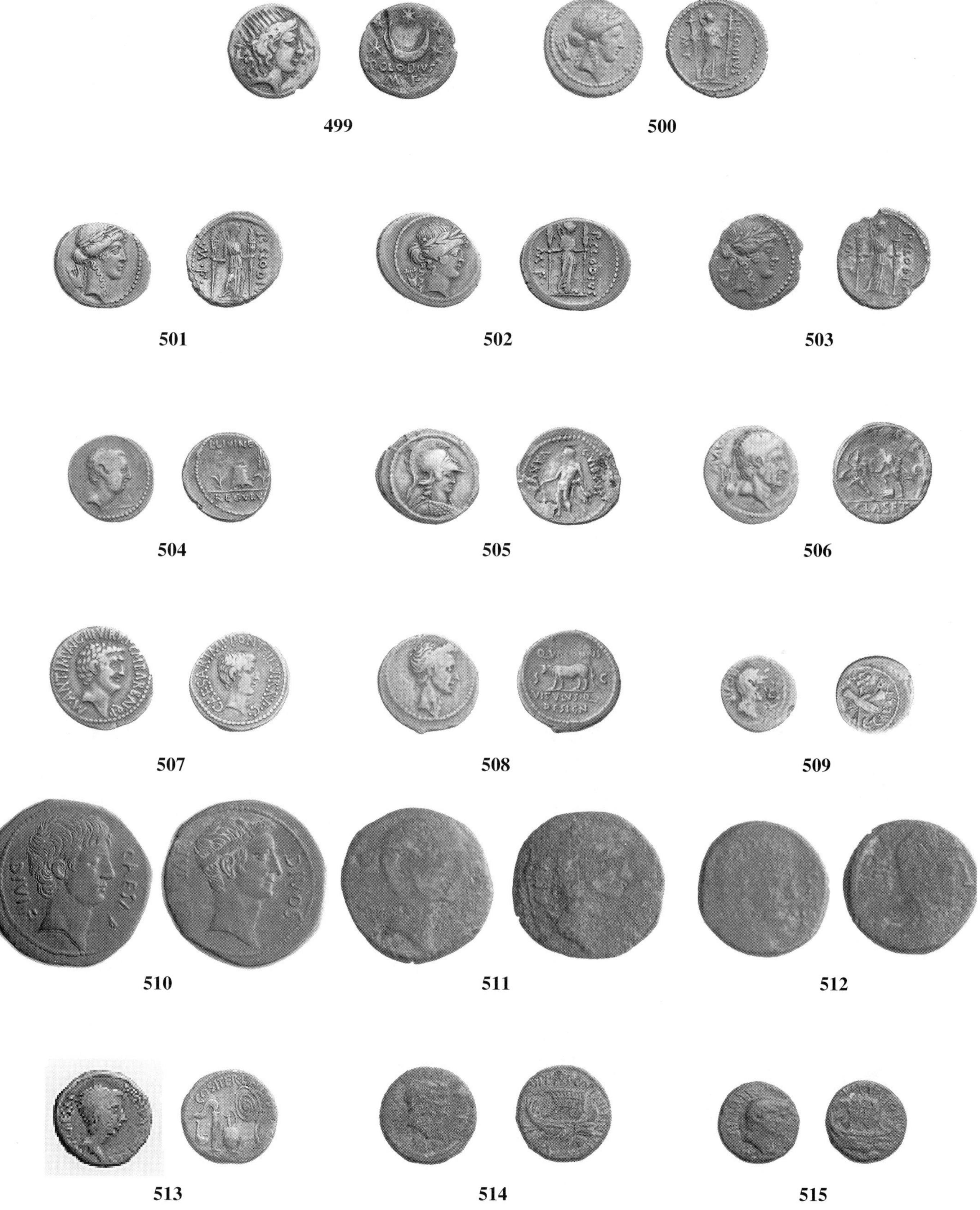

499

500

501

502

503

504

505

506

507

508

509

510

511

512

513

514

515

516   517   518

519   520   521

522   523   524

APPENDIX A

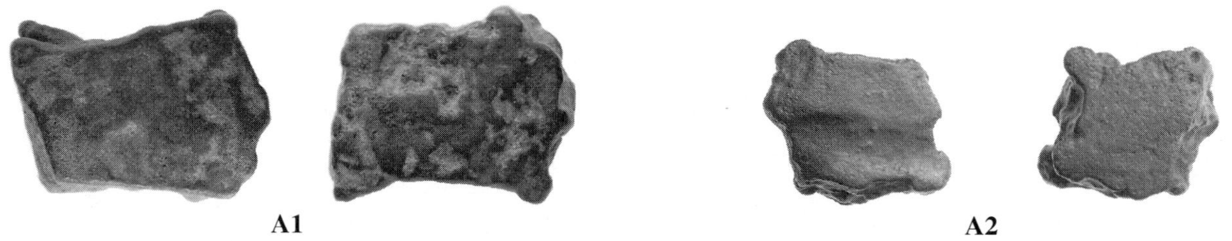

A1   A2

APPENDIX B

B1   B2

B3

B4

B5

APPENDIX C

C1

C2

C3

INDEXES

INDEX I OBVERSE TYPES

INDEX II REVERSE TYPES

INDEX III LATIN AND GREEK LEGENDS (EXCLUDING CONTROL LETTERS)